The Intellectual Capital of Schools

Measuring and Managing Knowledge, Responsibility and Reward: Lessons from the Commercial Sector

by

Anthony Kelly

*University of Southampton,
United Kingdom*

KLUWER ACADEMIC PUBLISHERS

DORDRECHT / BOSTON / LONDON

A C.I.P. Catalogue record for this book is available from the Library of Congress.

ISBN 1-4020-1932-7 (HB)
ISBN 1-4020-1935-1 (PB)

Published by Kluwer Academic Publishers,
P.O. Box 17, 3300 AA Dordrecht, The Netherlands.

Sold and distributed in North, Central and South America
by Kluwer Academic Publishers,
101 Philip Drive, Norwell, MA 02061, U.S.A.

In all other countries, sold and distributed
by Kluwer Academic Publishers,
P.O. Box 322, 3300 AH Dordrecht, The Netherlands.

Printed on acid-free paper

Printed in the Netherlands.

In memory of my father

CONTENTS

PREFACE

> A teacher may get good, even astounding, results from his pupils while he is teaching them and yet not be a good teacher; because it may be that, while his pupils are directly under his influence, he raises them to a height which is not natural to them, without fostering their own capacities for work at this level, so that they immediately decline again as soon as the teacher leaves the classroom.
>
> *Ludwig Wittgenstein, 1889 – 1951.*

It is difficult to measure effectiveness in not-for-profit organisations like schools, colleges and universities. There is no 'bottom-line' against which to gauge performance, they have limited technical development and managers struggle to make meaningful comparisons between outcomes and targets. In education, well-publicised attempts have been made to establish - some would say impose - a set of criteria by which organisations judge success or failure. These have been largely subjective - the percentage of inspected classes regarded as good, the extent to which staff is involved in decision making, the appropriateness of the leadership shown by senior managers, and so on – if occasionally peppered with quantitative measures, like the percentage of students achieving certain grades in public examinations, to sustain the illusion of objectivity. This is not to fault the aspiration necessarily, though initially at least it created a surveillance culture in schools that did justice to neither the inspected nor the argument for inspection.

Happily, this is changing. School inspection is now more centred on improvement than blame; on critical friendship more than confrontation. But the fundamental difficulty remains: how do educational organisations gauge an improvement in the value they add to the processes for which they are responsible?

Attempts at a resolution have so far centred on measuring external stakeholder outcomes - examination results, parental satisfaction and inspection grades - but have failed to capture the essence of what it is to be, or what it takes to become, a successful improving school. This book is an attempt to approach the problem from a different angle: namely, by describing the potential for improvement in terms of a school's internal intellectual capital; not so much to measure it (which may be impossible anyway) as to manage it and facilitate its development.

Education is about adding value to schooling. Since student and parent populations are by definition transient, the greatest potential long-term resource at the disposal of a school is its collective experience and expertise, and the competencies of its teaching staff. These assets must be put to best use (and not just good use) if schools are to operate at their full potential.

So what is 'capital' in the sense in which it is used in this book? There are many definitions and many types - intellectual, social, cultural, financial, structural and physical, to name but a few - and recently an attempt has been made to link some of them together in terms that relate to educational outcomes (Hargreaves, 2001, 2003). *Capital* is the knowledge and utility that comes from the interactions that inevitably arise when people work and learn together. Hence, the *socio-cultural capital* of schools is the knowledge that comes from the social and cultural interactions that result from having people educated together; the *physical capital* of schools includes the value that is added to the process of schooling by the equipment and built environment of the school. They are both vital elements in education and schooling processes, but they are largely outside the control of individual school managers. They are externally imposed and have well-defined extrinsic restrictions on what managers can do with them.

Intellectual capital on the other hand is at the core of what society deems to be the purpose and definition of successful schooling. It is the resource that comes from relationships between the school and its stakeholders, from the school's ability to innovate and manage change, from its infrastructure, and from the knowledge, experience and transferable competencies of its staff. Being largely internal to the organisation, it promises maximum leverage in the search for educational improvement and schooling effectiveness. And it is what this book is all about.

There is a puritanical tendency in education to adopt improvement measures that cause pain in the belief that they alone can be right. This book attempts no such flagellation. It concentrates on intellectual capital in the belief that while other forms of capital are important, they are ancillary to the core purpose of schooling as defined by society and as pursued by the state. It is for others to form their own typological constructions; the concentration here is on the form of capital which (it is thought) makes the greatest difference to educational outcomes and which can most easily be manipulated by managers towards that end.

The book is laid out in eight chapters: Chapter 1 introduces the concept of intellectual capital as it has come to us from new-economy commercial companies and extends it for use in schools; Chapter 2 constructs a typology for intellectual capital, its flows and measures; Chapter 3 outlines the theory of responsibility measurement, describing salaried and hourly-rated jobs, and the totality of work; Chapter 4 describes a Guide Chart method for job evaluation (with examples) and makes the case for job appraisal; Chapter 6 introduces knowledge continuity management and how schools can best retain whatever intellectual capital they have developed; Chapter 7 (drawn from case studies of good practice) describes how knowledge continuity can best be managed, how a school's critical processes can be identified and prioritised through the process of knowledge continuity audits, and how a school can be reshaped as a network of issue-centred teams; and Chapter 8 constructs some intellectual capital metrics to identify, analyse and exploit knowledge work and value creation.

CHAPTER 1

Introduction to the concept of intellectual capital

> Mankind has a great aversion to intellectual labour; but even supposing knowledge to be easily attainable, more people would be content to be ignorant than would take even a little trouble to acquire it.
>
> *Samuel Johnson, 1709 - 1784.*

INTRODUCTION

Capital, at its most basic, is the wealth that an organisation has at its disposal to carry out its functions. Traditionally, it is the sum of an organisation's resources and is its primary source of influence and competitive advantage in the marketplace. *Intellectual capital*, in particular, is the capital resource that comes from relationships between stakeholders and partners, from an organisation's ability to innovate and manage change, from its infrastructure, and from the knowledge, experience and transferable competencies of its staff. It has been described as a language for thinking and doing something about an organisation's potential for adding value (Roos et al., 1997) and in recent years it has considerably increased its role in the value-creation process. In part at least, this is due to fundamental changes in society and the global economy, where services have replaced manufacturing and production as the primary source of wealth in what has become known as the post-Fordist era (Piore & Sabel, 1984; Block, 1990; Reich, 1991). Knowledge is now acknowledged as the most important resource an organisation has, and a company's value – in other words, what stakeholders think of it - reflects the market's perception of how well knowledge management is integrated into the organisation proper.

The problem of measuring the value added by a school in the education process has been something of a holy grail for education policy-makers and researchers in recent times. If the extent of a school's contribution (or lack of it) to student achievement could be quantified, it would immediately resolve all problems of accountability.

While the concept of intellectual capital does not offer such a denouement, it does represent a fusion between the two different theoretical perspectives that have traditionally sought to make a contribution to such a resolution; one that focuses on generating and exploiting knowledge and intangibles in the manner of *school improvement* and one that focuses on measuring output in terms of determinants in the manner of *school effectiveness*.

The perspective of school improvement has two facets. In one, the school as an entity is regarded as the unit of study, innovation and expertise are things that are typically imported from outside, and the focus is on organisational outcomes. In the other, the focus is on individual processes; a bottom-up approach that is based on the expertise of practitioners (Teddlie & Reynolds, 2000). From both points of view, the primary concern is to discover what makes some schools effective and others not, and how that situation changes over time. The perspective is largely idiographic.

The perspective of school effectiveness, on the other hand, concentrates on the empirical measurement of outcomes and describes the attributes of effective schools in a nomothetic sense. Like the school improvement perspective, the focus is on the organisation rather than on the individual.

The concepts that underpin intellectual capital mirror both these perspectives, but to understand its nature it is important to distinguish between its different forms and how they metamorphose from one to another. It is the purpose of intellectual capital management, an amalgam of school improvement and school effectiveness approaches, to understand and manage the dynamics of these flows.

The management of intellectual capital in schools should have its foundation in strategy, since it is only possible to measure effectiveness against the strategic objectives of an organisation. There are no universally accepted objective measures of what makes a school 'good'; no single descriptor that is appropriate to all scenarios. Strategic objectives are the only sensible guide to the selection of appropriate indicators for measuring the forms and flows of intellectual capital that are deemed important. Since to capture progress, these indicators must eventually be coalesced into a single overall index, they should be coherent with the strategic aims.

There is not likely to be a shortage of suitable intellectual capital indicators; the tricky thing for a school's senior management team is to be able to reduce them to a few important ones, which despite the simplification, still constitute a rigorous description and measurement of the intellectual capital of the school.

THE POST-INDUSTRIAL BUSINESS ENVIRONMENT

Traditionally, the assets of a commercial organisation were measured only in terms of its production and plant - its *hard assets*. The most highly valued companies were the ones that kept production turn-around time to a minimum, balanced stock and sales, got the best return on financial reserves, and hedged investments to provide a prudent mixture of debt and security for the future. For schools, this meant measuring worth in terms of examination results, university entrance success, pupil enrolment trends, pupil-teacher ratios, the quality of its built environment, value for money, and staff recruitment, retention and development.

In the new economy, by contrast, the most highly prized companies are the ones that best manage intangibles, such as the ability to generate value and intellectual capital, rather than hard assets. Software companies such as Microsoft, for example, are valued more highly than their hard assets would suggest under traditional methods of reckoning. They are perceived by the market to be worth more than product-based companies, despite having fewer and less valuable hard assets.

The fact that there is a difference between the perceived (for-sale) market value of a company and its hard-asset (book) value is nothing new of course. The difference has for a long time been incorporated into accounting practices under the euphemism 'goodwill'. What is different today is the size of that hidden value, particularly in software companies and companies with high-visibility brands,[1] and the degree of expectation on the part of the market that companies manage intangibles just as they do other assets. It is hard to gauge exactly what proportion of a commercial company's value comes from hidden value-creators like customer relations, in-house expertise, experience and competencies, brands and the potential for new products, and how much comes from traditional hard assets, but it is clear that invisible assets generate a very significant amount of wealth and that the market expects them be managed in a commensurately serious fashion.

This new commercial paradigm has yet fully to impinge on schools, but schooling (as opposed to education) eventually goes the way of economics because schooling is largely a society-sponsored activity. And for once, this is good news for school-based professionals. If ever there was a cohort of organisations in need of intellectual capital management, it is schools. The irony will not be lost on headteachers that, in future, businesses will have to be managed like education should have been in the past; and in this respect schools will be expected to follow the lead given by commercial companies!

Intellectual capital represents the potential within an organisation for generating value as well as being an asset in the traditional sense. It is the new imperative of management to manage invisible assets, so the concept of intellectual capital implies more than just knowledge about the competencies of employees; it implies some kind of practicum as well. In the post-Fordist economy, where the principal agent for change is not so much marketplace globalisation as the way information determines the progress of enterprise, knowledge and information are the most important routes to improvement. Despite the hype, globalisation is not the defining feature of the new economy; markets were always global for some organisations, even as far back as the Seventeenth century.[2] What is different now is that information is no longer precious, the possession of the privileged professional few, but freely available to everyone and available in real time.

The inherent value of the Internet and improved worldwide communications technology lies in the twin innovations of access and speed. Technological advances in the way information is stored and processed has both caused and facilitated change. Modern computers can process data at such speed and at such relatively low cost that knowledge is now more widely available and access to it more routine. Furthermore, better communications technology has diminished the significance of geographical location; the world has simply become a smaller place. Financial factors affecting one region can now more easily affect what happens in another, as surely as weather

---

[1] In 2003, Philip Morris (Marlboro), Coca Cola (Coke) and Anheuser Busch (Budweiser) were reckoned, in that order, to be the world's most valuable brands, but other companies spring to mind; Levi Strauss (casual jeans), Nike (sportswear), and so on.
[2] Lloyds Insurance Company, for example, was founded in 1688 to insure ships and cargo for a worldwide market.

patterns. The ripples of accounting scandals in the USA are immediately felt in stock markets from London to Tokyo, notwithstanding the time differential.[3] And of course, there is a much greater demand for information today, due to increased customer sophistication and a better-educated and more demanding public, which in turn has helped to shift Western economies from a manufacturing to a service base.

Education too has developed a more sophisticated customer base and within reason, geographical separation is nowadays less of a barrier to choosing a preferred school. In addition, parents and students now have access at minimal cost to information that would previously have been confined to teachers and heads, or would have been expensive and troublesome to obtain. And of course the fact that schools are now more closely linked to each other - by sector, by government initiative and by research - means that what one school achieves affects how others are perceived.

The ease and speed with which information is obtained is not the only difference between the old and new economies. Something of more fundamental importance has changed. New economy companies now follow a law of *increasing* returns. The traditional law of diminishing returns, formulated at the end of the 19th century, states that the greater the quantity of a thing in supply (whether property, capital or labour) the less valuable it is, and consequently the biggest profits come from the least exploited resources. Companies that are regulated according to this economic rubric - in other words, companies that obey a law of negative feedback - are in a natural equilibrium state and when an equilibrium is broken, negative feedback cycles return them to a new equilibrium. In a typical scenario sequence, expansion of production initially lowers cost and price by spreading the cost of production over more units, but limited natural resources eventually mean that production must resort to lower-yield sources in order to continue, thus reversing (partially at least) the effect of lower prices. Thus a new unique equilibrium is created.[4]

In new economy companies, negative feedback economics are reversed (Arthur, 1990; Wysocki, 1994). They operate in a paradigm of *positive* feedback economics. Nowadays, the *more* of something that is created, the greater the returns generated. Companies operating according to laws of increasing returns, typically high-tech companies, have relatively high development costs and relatively low production costs. They are regulated according to positive feedback economics and do not react in the same way as traditional companies; their market equilibriums are unstable (Kelly, 2003) and it becomes virtually impossible to predict which equilibrium will eventually dominate. In such a scenario, the value of products (and hence the value of the companies themselves) lies in how widespread is their usage. Think of the VHS / Betamax competition in the early Eighties, or that between Microsoft and Apple a decade later. The system that wins out is not necessarily the better product technologically, but the one that most quickly gets locked into the market. It becomes too risky for end-users to go against the prevailing popular trend, and too costly in terms of re-equipment and re-training for them to change their minds later because of the effort required in re-familiarisation. In the case of the Microsoft / Apple

---

[3] For example, in May and June 2002, the accounting scandals at energy trader Enron, telecommunications giant WorldCom and photocopier company Xerox had an immediate and devastating impact on the world's stock markets. Compare this to the two or three days it took the fallout from the 1929 Wall Street crash to reach London.

[4] Mining ore that is less and less pure, or less easily accessed, is one example. The savings made by producing a greater quantity are eventually balanced by the increased costs involved.

competition, for example, IBM supported Microsoft's DOS system and licensed clones of its own machines to be built by other companies. Apple did not, and despite being widely perceived as the technically superior product, its role was soon reduced to that of a minority player in a market it had previously dominated. Microsoft DOS simply got greater diffusion. Software engineers wrote more DOS-compatible programmes and more DOS systems were sold because customers opted for the safer, more popular, system.

Some indication of the importance of fast market lock-in can be got by looking at how precipitate is usually the introduction of new computer software products to the market, even when flawed with bugs. 'Hit the market quickly' is the new mantra, and the consequences of getting even the slightest edge in that respect have a cumulative effect on dominance. Positive feedback economic loops amplify the slightest advantage over competitors and it takes a lot to reverse a market lead in such a situation. Consumers opt for products that merely *suggest* future dominance and that in itself becomes a self-fulfilling prophecy. Widespread sales of the product that is perceived to lead the market mean that related products must be made compatible, which in turn locks the market into a position that ensures dominance over the competition. Under these conditions, forecasting becomes nigh impossible, but paradoxically, the prize of market dominance goes to the company that can best guess the shape of the future. So although forecasting becomes more difficult, it becomes more important, and with optimisation so difficult given the multitude of possible equilibrium points, the best organisations can hope for is to be prepared for change.

Of course, not all of this is applicable to schools and their management. The change to a law of increasing returns, for example, is a purely economic concept and has little application to education. Nevertheless, school managers and governors will find resonance with some of the scenarios described above. In schools, as elsewhere, the uncertainty of the market, the pace of change and the instability of equilibriums make it difficult to predict the future and plan strategically for it. Additionally, the issue of market lock-in is sometimes a scenario experienced by schools struggling to reverse a declining enrolment trend against more successful competitors. As in the commercial sector, it is an issue of stakeholder confidence; parents choose schools on the basis of what can be termed *reasonable expectation*. If a school is perceived as successful, parents get locked into it as a place of first choice because the alternative is perceived as having greater risk attached to it, or at any rate as something requiring disproportionately more effort to achieve the same degree of familiarisation. And like for-profit companies, schools that can best guess the shape of the future are best placed to enjoy it. Those organisations will be the ones that best manage their intellectual capital.

A word of caution: it is possible that the economics of increasing returns only constitute a transition phase for the market (Arthur, 1996). As industries mature, return per unit of production might once again diminish as output increases. They may be following a curve like that in Figure 1, which increases initially as the product is used more, only to slow down later. It is known that some products pass through an increasing return phase and stabilise later on the laws of diminishing return, but it is not yet known whether new technology industries are following a similar pattern.[5]

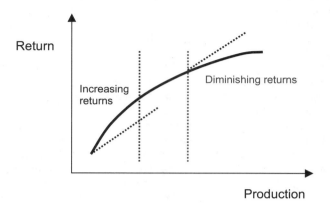

Figure 1. Curve showing a relative decrease in return as the organisation matures

MANAGING INTELLECTUAL CAPITAL

As the foregoing theoretical discussion suggests, the practicalities of managing intellectual capital are complicated by the fact that intangible assets seem to obey different economic laws to those of traditional, hard, visible assets. For one thing, employees can be both a decreasing and an increasing return factor, depending on whether they are regarded as labour or as a source of knowledge respectively. If management is to realise the full intellectual potential of its workforce, it must be prepared to alter its way of thinking. As it measures the hidden value of the organisation, it must come to regard its collective knowledge and experience as sources of sustainable competitive advantage. Today, organisational knowledge has to be managed, not necessarily in the same way as traditional assets, but for similar reasons.

As already mentioned, the creation of a comprehensive system to describe and measure the intellectual capital of an organisation (and its flows) must be rooted in the organisation's strategy. Strategy and strategy alone should determine the indicators most appropriate to the measurement of intellectual capital, because it is strategy that defines the forms and flows of intellectual capital that are deemed most important by (and to) the organisation. When it comes to the practicality of actually choosing the indicators, there is little point compiling a long list of them without any prioritisation, because that would make it impossible thereafter to evaluate outcomes or compare benefits. Conversely, there is little point having intellectual capital indicators that bear no relation at all to the everyday operational side of the organisation. A balance must be found; indicators should be relatively few in number, yet capture the essence of

---

[5] The economics of increasing returns applies not just to new technology industries, but to all knowledge-intensive organisations. However, it does not apply in the same way to all intangibles. Brands, for example, increase their value with use, but can easily be ruined by a single badly judged extension.

what employees do and be rooted in the organisation's strategy. Finally, having selected and refined a set of intellectual capital indicators, a weighted index can then be compiled that assigns to each a weight that reflects its importance to the company's strategic scheme and consolidates them all into a single measurement. Not all indicators will be equally important; some will have a greater impact on the organisation's mission than others and will therefore be more heavily weighted.

In general, intellectual capital indices should be:

- Sensitive, but not overly so. They should be able to respond to changes fairly quickly, but not be so sensitive that they react unduly to the small temporary fluctuations that are a natural part of corporate life.
- Accurate, insofar as they should be able to differentiate between levels of change and degrees of success.
- Reliable in that they do actually measure what they purport to measure.

Managing intellectual capital and responding to change

One of the essential skills of intellectual capital management is the ability to manage and respond quickly to change, something that is more easily achieved within what Senge (1990), Garratt (2000) and others have called a 'learning organisation'. In his book *The Fifth Discipline: the art and practice of the learning organisation*, Senge outlined the five disciplines or *competent technologies* that underpin the idea of an organisation in which innovative patterns of thinking are nurtured and learning to learn is encouraged. What distinguishes such organisations from traditional controlling ones is their mastery of these five basic disciplines: the discipline of continually clarifying its mission and its future; the discipline of challenging ingrained assumptions that influence how people think and act; the discipline of sharing visions and motivating others; the discipline of learning in teams; and the discipline of systems thinking, the 'fifth discipline' that gave its name to the book and which Senge suggests underpins the other four. And what distinguishes leadership in such organisations from traditional leadership is its transformational nature - its metanoia - based on designing, stewarding and teaching: designing the organisation's policies, strategies and systems, and understanding how they fit together as a coherent whole; stewarding the vision and ensuring that it is broadly shared and universally adapted; teaching others to focus on purpose; and fostering a systemic understanding of the organisation. The link with intellectual capital and the management of intangibles is obvious: in a traditional controlling organisation, people only learn what they know they need to learn; in a learning organisation, committed to the management of its intellectual capital, they learn how to learn.

Michael Fullan's (1991) seminal work, *The New Meaning of Educational Change*, imported much of Senge's work to education and interpreted it for schools. In education, professionals need to attach personal meaning to experience, and initiatives need to be assimilated over time before meaning can be shared. The impetus for change in organisations might come from small groups, but the momentum to sustain it comes from a *bias for action* within the whole organisation. Change needs both pressure and support to sustain it. For teachers, that means that they must develop a collaborative culture that converts tacit knowledge to explicit knowledge, while being cautious about what Andy Hargreaves (1992) has termed 'contrived collegiality'. For headteachers, that means coping with the chaos and conflict that is inherent in school management; pulled towards stability by collegiality and towards instability by

individualism. Success in managing intellectual capital in schools lies in maintaining
the organisation on the cusp of both.

Competition and cooperation

First move and fast response confer a huge advantage in a positive feedback situation.
It can turn a small advantage into market dominance in a short period of time. Layers
of middle management are a barrier to success in this respect. Whether or not such
barriers exist in an organisation depends on circumstance as much as corporate
intention or style of leadership. Organisational maturity, size, operational
requirements all have an influence, but what is certain is that layers of middle
management whose existence serves only to buffer leadership from the
unpleasantness of decision making and provide a comfort zone for those at either end
of the responsibility spectrum, can have no place in a competitive organisation.

Cooperation within and without an organisation can offer a route to improvement too.
Today, for commercial companies, success in the market place can more easily be
achieved in partnership with like organisations than was the case in the past, because
knowledge-based enterprises are more closely related to each other and to each
other's activities than manufacturing enterprises. This is particularly true in education
generally, despite the fact that cooperation is massively under-exploited as a result of
an externally imposed accountability structure that pits schools against each other
without conferring any real advantage on the consumer. The league-table compliance
mentality that currently prevails in education, in the UK at least, serves to actively
discourage cooperation. A high-achieving school helping an under-performing one
guarantees only to pull itself back towards the median and has little incentive to
cooperate. Notwithstanding the present situation, there are many possible areas for
cooperation between schools, and between schools and commercial organisations, that
can (and need to) be exploited in the future (Kelly, 2001). Schools driven by an
intellectual capital outlook will look for them.

There is a psychological aspect to competition and cooperation, which is seldom
taken into account by managers and rarely understood. In the commercial sector, if
competitors believe that a product is already locked into a market, they are more
reluctant to engage the fray than if the market is open. Premature announcements of
breakthrough products and upbeat trading and research statements are favourite tactics
in this *game of market exploitation* (Rapoport, 1967; Kelly, 2003).[6] The most

---

[6] Games with a certain type of pay-off matrix are called *games of exploitation* (Kelly, 2003) because
players who deviate unilaterally from the safe minimax strategy benefit themselves at the expense of
the other players. In going after the best possible pay-off, the deviant risks disaster for everyone.
It is imperative in games of exploitation that players who intend to deviate from the minimax strategy
convince other players that they are resolute in their intent. Put crudely, the most convincing player
always wins exploitation games. And the more games of this sort a player wins, the more likely the
player is to continue winning, since the player's seriousness of intent has been amply demonstrated and
the player becomes more confident. Reputation - the sum of a player's historical behaviour in previous
trials of the game - is everything. As Colman (1982) put it, 'nothing succeeds like success in the field
of brinkmanship'. The more reckless, selfish and irrational players are perceived to be, the greater is
their advantage, since opposing players know that they risk disaster if they try to win. This
psychological use of craziness can be seen in terrorist organisations (Corsi, 1981), and among political
leaders and small children.

convincing 'player' always wins and the more games of this sort a player wins, the more likely the player is to continue winning. Reputation - the sum of a player's historical behaviour - is very important in competitive situations.

Today, managers must manage all the assets of a company and not just the visible, tangible ones. In fact, against today's paradigm it is difficult to justify the prominence given to the management of financial assets, since they are merely a consequence of something else; it is part of a natural inclination to concentrate attention on managing those assets which are easily quantified and headline-grabbing. Managers of intellectual capital should avoid this, though that might require a deeper strategic approach than is the norm and a fundamental shift in perspective. Traditionally, managers dislike uncertainty and change, but uncertainty and change have become the unavoidable lot of those who seek to maximise organisational effectiveness in the new paradigm. As Roos et al. (1997) put it:

> *"Managers (will) have to resort to navigation instead of planning. Abandoning all hope of going straight towards the goals, managers (will) need to learn to set a clear direction and then stay as close to it as they can. It is not an easy task."* (p.14).

A THEORY OF INTELLECTUAL CAPITAL FOR SCHOOLS

Over the last number of years, as the importance of knowledge management has increased in the commercial sector, various theories of management have been developed to underpin its practice. Some of these have now coalesced to form the concept of intellectual capital, but two distinct schools of thought are still recognisable within it, which have parallels in education: a *Knowledge Improvement* approach and a *Knowledge Effectiveness* approach (see Figure 2). The former concentrates on knowledge generation and utilisation; the latter on measurement and the link between it and output.

It should be noted that, although deviant players are perceived to be irrational, they are nevertheless acting rationally throughout, given their purpose in winning the game. (Schelling, 1960; Howard, 1966; Brams, 1975).

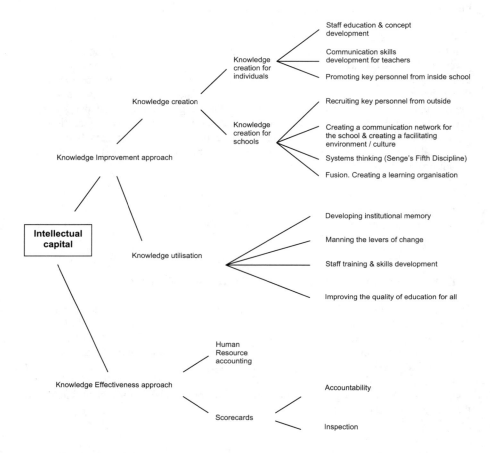

Figure 2. A theory of intellectual capital for schools showing two distinct approaches

Knowledge improvement and utilisation

The Knowledge Improvement approach focuses sometimes on knowledge creation and sometimes on knowledge utilisation: how individual teacher knowledge and corporate school knowledge is generated, and how experience is used through teaching and management competencies to add value to the processes undertaken by the school. Senge's (1990) concept of five organisational disciplines falls into the category of knowledge creation, whereas work in the United Kingdom by Hargreaves (1990), Ainscow et al (1994) and others, has concentrated on knowledge utilisation, capacity building and how best to leverage improvement in schools.

A school can develop expertise organically and internally through staff development, or by importing it through targeted recruitment. The latter approach is the one favoured by government and local education authorities for failing schools because its effect is immediate. In theory, the imported *übermensch* - usually a new headteacher or curriculum manager; less frequently a pastoral leader - brings expertise to the school that did not exist there previously, or at least not in sufficient quantity, and trickles it down through the organisation with the aim of transforming its moribund culture. It is a far from inexpensive approach to an emergency situation, though the extent to which a school and its teachers benefit from it in the long-term is less certain. Much depends on the accuracy of the local authority's assessment of the school's perceived needs in the first place, and the extent to which the recruits possess the right skills.

Internal staff development is expensive too. It is usually spread over a protracted period of time involving large numbers of staff. It is a commitment rather than an undertaking and much depends on the thoroughness of its design, the quality of its delivery and how well integrated it is (Mortimore et al., 1988).
Many schools bring in outside consultants to conduct their training and development sessions, while ignoring the more obvious and accessible asset of existing staff expertise. External consultants are not always successful (Levine & Lezotte, 1990). The cult of the education guru might serve to entertain the troops at the end of a stressful year teaching, but there is no evidence to link it with enhanced performance or the widespread development of new competencies among staff. At the very least, schools should combine their approaches to staff development, using in-house personnel to spread good practice whenever possible.

Whichever approach to knowledge creation is chosen, it is useful to construct a typology of knowledge types. The simplest one categorises knowledge as either *tacit* or *explicit* (Polanyi, 1956), though an autopoietic view of epistemology would dispute such a dichotomy, holding that all knowledge is necessarily private and tacit and that explicit knowledge is by definition merely data (Varela, Thompson & Rosch, 1992). Explicit knowledge can be fully described and stored in transmittable algorithmic form, whereas tacit knowledge is individual and personal to its holder. When there is a transfer from one category to another (see Figure 3), additional knowledge is generated:
- Tacit - Tacit transfers generate additional internal knowledge through critical reflection, a defining characteristic of teaching as a profession (Schön, 1983).
- Tacit - Explicit transfers generate knowledge through research, its dissemination to practitioner audiences and the documentation of own experience.
- Explicit - Tacit transfers are what define a change in the actual practice of teaching, effected by codifying the experiences of others and personalising them.
- There can be no Explicit - Explicit transfers because knowledge cannot be generated by or transferred between computers or documents without a human intermediary.

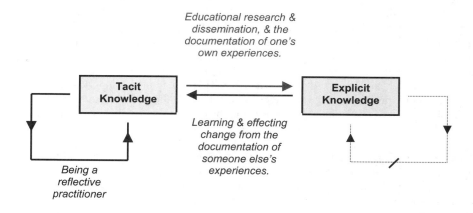

Figure 3. The transfer and generation of knowledge: a simple typology

All forms of knowledge-transfer involve the coming together of individuals in some form or other. As Roos et al (1997) point out; without sharing, knowledge cannot be created. So the essential task of intellectual capital management is what could be called *fusion* - bringing people together in a deliberate manipulation to create knowledge - and the key to its success is good communications. A good corporate communication network facilitates the generation and retention of intellectual capital, allows it to affect practice with a view to improvement and makes transparent any critical assessment of its effect on outcomes.

In schools, developing good communication skills in individual teachers is generally less problematic than developing a good corporate environment for communication.[7] It is in the nature of things that good teachers tend to have highly developed communication skills, but the extent to which teachers actually communicate with each other depends, not on their own innate ability to do so, but on the availability of formal communication frameworks. In this and similar ways, the theory and practical management of intellectual capital is inextricably linked to the organisational discipline of systems thinking; much depends on creating an environment in which vision and mastery are shared and professionalism invigorated.

On a practical level, there are many measures that can be taken to develop effective communication networks in schools, though they are only cosmetic unless a culture of sharing is first developed:

- There should be formal structures for sharing knowledge. Staff meetings, in-service days and off-campus training are essential at all levels.
- Agenda items should be categorised for staff meetings according to importance. Not everything warrants a full discussion; some items should be 'for information' only. Research has shown that generally, teachers find staff

---

[7] The term 'corporate' is used deliberately here since what is being said can apply equally to individual schools, groups of schools within a local education authority or indeed groups of local authorities.

meetings endlessly circuitous and are frustrated by the amount of time spent needlessly discussing that which cannot be changed (Angeleides, 2003). The simplest method of categorisation is to asterisk some items 'for information' and others 'for discussion'.

- Staff should be afforded structured opportunities for casual communication. In the new mathematics faculty building at the University of Cambridge, for example, canteen tables have writing surfaces. A more common approach is to place water fountains strategically with a view to encouraging social interaction.

- A well-designed and well-equipped teachers' common room is essential. Newspapers and professional journals should be provided; radios and televisions avoided. Internet access should be confined to a designated location and limited during common break times.

- Open-plan offices help break down the cellular structures of isolation, but it is important to provide privacy for individuals in such environments. In staff common rooms, for example, a certain level of background noise - not too intrusive - is a good thing so that staff can speak to each other without being overheard.

- Junior teachers should be encouraged to the difficult task of sharing opinions and engaging in critical discussion with senior colleagues. Experience suggests that this is easier, in the initial stages at least, in informal settings. Perhaps surprisingly, input from newly appointed staff is often most valuable in relation to strategic matters, where they have least experience, because they carry less professional and political 'baggage' to the discussion.

Most teachers have a natural inclination, in school at least, towards social interaction, so communication management in schools is usually more a case of facilitating a natural inclination than seeking an unnatural reversal. Headteachers must avail of every opportunity to open communication networks within and without the school for the benefit of staff, no matter how counter-intuitive it might seem to encourage what appears at first sight to be frivolity. The meta-skill of learning how to learn, which transforms experience into learning, is a skill that is very difficult to transfer among colleagues, so despite the fact that every instance of non-directive communication entails some loss of structure, heads and deputies should strive not to curtail involvement, but to steer it. Otherwise there can be no sharing of vision and therefore no leadership, only management.

The utilisation of knowledge created by the measures and circumstances described above is a necessary step in the Knowledge Improvement approach to the management of intellectual capital. To effect positive change and add value to the education processes for which a school is responsible, created knowledge must be applied to the everyday operations of the school. Over time and through development and research, the intellectual capital that best effects positive variance in performance accumulates in the organisation's reservoir of experience. For this to generate yet more intellectual capital there must be some form of institutional memory; that is, some systemic mechanism by which practical knowledge is codified and stored for future use. Sadly - because in most other respects, it is an inspiring experience for all concerned - one of the great disadvantages of charismatic leadership is its inability to develop such mechanisms. Experience has shown how paltry is the organisational legacy left behind when a charismatic headteacher moves on, and how difficult it is for those who remain to add to what has gone before.

Knowledge effectiveness and measurement

The measurement of intangibles is by definition difficult and inexact - the 'bean counters' have long since despaired of it - but some progress has been made as a result of increased customer awareness and the market's demand for better quality goods as standard (Eccles, 1991; Fornell, 1992). The introduction of measurement systems that purport to gauge changes in the format and quality of intellectual capital or any other intangible asset must be preceded by a strategic decision on what indicators should be used. As far as schools are concerned, much depends on what is deemed valuable at the time and where improvement is most urgently needed; examination results, teacher recruitment and retention, satisfaction among parents, student attendance, or whatever. Measurement is always a judgement-laded exercise.

Different sections within the school organisation will have different data requirements for their indicators, and indeed this is probably a good thing, but there should also be some overarching indicators for whole-school evaluation to avoid 'balkanisation'. The general rule for intellectual capital indicators in schools is that they should be flexible enough to adapt to department-specific requirements and changing demands, yet be capable of facilitating institution-wide discussion.

Having decided what to measure and why, the next move is to decide how to measure it. This is largely a question of resource allocation. Nothing kills enthusiasm quite like lack of support, so initial management estimates should err on the side of generosity when it comes to providing administrative and ICT support and classroom cover for involved staff. To make an accurate assessment of what is needed, there must first be an accurate assessment of what exists, so an audit of relevant tangible and intangible resources within the school should be made. This should be done *after* deciding what is required from the measurement exercise; if the audit is done first, there is a tendency to 'cut the suit to fit the cloth'.

It can be helpful to provide a catalogue of sources of help available. For secondary schools, this list might include local universities and institutes of higher education, local education authorities, local and national curriculum associations, headteacher and teacher associations, local voluntary organisations and businesses, parents and students. Meaningful assessment cannot be achieved 'on the cheap'. If the audit throws up glaring deficits, outside expertise will have to be bought in. Managers must be prepared for that; there is no shame in it. If there were no shortcomings, there would be no improvement.

While the immediate aim is to measure how things are, the medium-term aim is to make things better and this usually requires a shift in emphasis as far as incentivisation is concerned. Teachers who are supportive of improvement initiatives are already likely to be hard working and conscientious, so they are probably working to capacity anyway. They do not need more work, just different work. For these and other staff, there must be linkage between desired organisational outcomes and personal esteem; if outcomes shift in importance, so too should promotion criteria. Management must be prepared to refocus incentives and promotion in such a way as to drive the organisation in the desired direction in an efficient manner. It is nonsensical to reward performance in an incidental area. Schools must be focused going forward and management must engage with the process knowing that difficult decisions lie ahead. The process of measurement needs the discipline of systems thinking, and organisations need to be geared to support it.

Organisations should adopt a multifaceted approach to compiling sets of intellectual capital indicators. They should be wide-ranging yet focused. They should seek to balance past and future performance, from the perspective of both internal and external stakeholders. The inclination to try to capture everything in one super-indicator should be resisted, as should the inclination to adopt a different indicator for every trivial aspect of organisational life.

Naturally, given the importance of examination results in the public's perception of effectiveness, schools tend to concentrate on them as indicators. This is fine as far as it goes, but just like commercial companies over-concentrating on financial reporting, it cannot tell the full story. Intellectual capital indicators for schools are not just about measuring examination success, because examinations only measure past achievement. Even the most ardent advocate of school league tables cannot have failed to notice how even highly-achieving schools fluctuate wildly in terms of performance and position over the space of a few years. This cannot reasonably be attributed to parallel fluctuations in teacher commitment or student ability; past examination success is not a reliable guide to future performance. Schools should include in their sets of indicators things like measures of growth in pupil numbers (as a percentage of catchment say), ratings of parent and staff satisfaction, information on staff turnover, statistics on income and expenditure per pupil and per examination grade, measures of added educational value, and so on.[8]

The most accurate snapshot of how things are and what remedial action needs to be taken over the short, medium and long terms, can be got from a balanced, multiple-focus, set of indicators (Kaplan & Norton, 1997). Critically, they must reflect the school's key strategies, and in addition should be:

- Relatively easy to use. Indicators that require degree-level mathematics or take too long to assemble are rarely worth the effort.
- Sensitive. They should be able to respond to changes fairly quickly, but should not be so sensitive that they over-react to small fluctuations.
- Accurate. They should be able to differentiate between levels of change and degrees of success.
- Reliable and valid. They should actually measure what they purport to measure.
- Attributable. They should be capable of making comparisons between departments within an organisation and between organisations; in other words, they should be capable of being isolated within departments or within organisations. Something that affects every department should not be chosen as an indicator for an individual department. Indicators should be peculiar to the area that they purport to measure.

While not every indicator will satisfy each of the above criteria in equal measure, managers should at least be aware of them (see Figure 4). Then, if and when action is

---

[8] The UK school league tables (January 2003) contain, for the first time, measures of added value. There are two measures for each school: one related to the progress made by pupils at the end of Key Stage 3; another related to the progress made by pupils at the end of compulsory schooling. They are discussed in greater detail in Chapter 8.

to be predicated upon one of them, a review can be undertaken to examine the case carefully in light of possible antecedent variables or contradictions.

Multiple-focus indicators

Indicator criteria	The extent to which the criteria are likely to be met in schools
Usability	Very likely. Teachers and school managers are professionals and (relatively) uniformly trained, and the indicators are likely to be mostly qualitative anyway.
Sensitivity	Fairly likely, but much depends on the indicators actually chosen. Some indicators only offer measurement on a post facto basis and so can be out of date by the time they are discussed with a view to effecting change.
Accuracy	Likely. Teachers and school managers are quick to spot even small deteriorations in student / parent / community response.
Reliability and validity	Unlikely. It is difficult in education to attribute causality to the many and varied influences that affect a pupil's progress in school.
Attributability	Likely. Teachers and school managers are relatively close to their 'customers' and while some indicators (such as pupil absenteeism) are 'whole-school', many others can be made specific to individual curriculum and management groupings.

Figure 4. Multiple-focus indicators and the likelihood of criteria being met in schools

More importantly, a timetable needs to be established that moves a set of indicators forward as the needs of a school evolve. This in turn can provoke new strategic initiatives and generate new indicators. Traditional timescales are not good enough. The demands made on schools change very quickly nowadays - almost daily it sometimes seems – and turnaround time has to be reduced to keep pace with that.

Constructing such a timetable requires a strategic review cycle like that represented by Figure 5, the results of which should be disseminated as part of a formal school inspection report or financial audit. Schools should follow the lead given by new-economy companies in the commercial sector and report on intellectual capital processes not traditionally shown on a balance sheet.[9] In the commercial sector, this is

---

[9] Skandia published the first report on intellectual capital in 1993, as a one-page section in its annual financial report. Dow Chemicals followed suit in 1996. According to Roos et al (1997), the US stock

now fairly standard practice; modern accounting methods increasingly take account of intangibles such as trademarks and patents. What is being advocated for schools is that they learn to report along similar lines; on intangibles such as reputation in the community, staff flexibility, acquired competencies such as the management of parent-teacher, teacher-pupil and community relations, experiential links with outside agencies such as examination boards, and so on. These are all dimensions of value creation in schools and form a legitimate part of the story they tell stakeholders, and by which they should ultimately be judged.

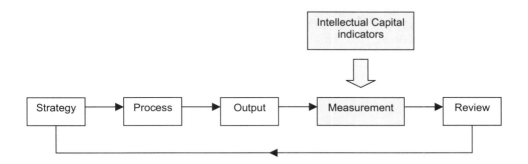

Figure 5. A strategic review cycle

Invisible assets generate organisational wealth. The flow of knowledge from one form to another or between a school and its environment generates intellectual capital, which is an amalgam of the school's knowledge, experience, organisational learning and competence. It needs to be built up gradually over time because experiential knowledge comprises a significant part of it. The more frequently it is manipulated or *mobilised* (Itami & Roehl, 1987), the more of it is generated and the greater its relative value to the organisation. Consequently, staff competencies that are critical to its production and retention need to be developed and managed so that they are integrated into the everyday practice of teaching and school leadership. Intellectual capital management is too important to be left to chance.

SUMMARY

Intellectual capital is the sum of the experience, knowledge and competence of staff. It is anything intangible that creates value and is the difference between the output of a school and its true worth. It comes from relationships between stakeholders and others, from a school's ability to innovate and manage change, from its organisational infrastructure, and from the expertise and transferable skills of its staff. Its

exchange watchdog, the Securities and Exchange Commission, has stated that in a few years' time it is likely that all companies quoted on Wall Street will be required to publish an intellectual capital report.

accumulated wealth is used to add value to the processes for which a school is held responsible.

Traditionally, value is measured only in terms of hard-assets like property, plant, stock and financial reserves. However, today, knowledge is the most important resource an organisation has and an organisation's value reflects the public's perception of how well knowledge management is integrated into the organisation proper. The most highly prized companies are the ones that best manage intangibles like intellectual capital.

It is hard to gauge exactly what proportion of organisational value stems from hidden value-creators, but it is clear that they generate wealth and an ever more sophisticated public expects them be managed, even if the practicalities of managing intellectual capital are complicated by the fact that intangible assets obey different economic laws to those of traditional, hard, visible assets. Education now has a more sophisticated customer base. Parents and students have access at minimal cost to information that was previously confined to teachers and heads, or previously had been expensive and troublesome to obtain, and the fact that schools are now more closely linked to each other means that what one school achieves affects how others are perceived.

The creation of a comprehensive system to describe and measure the intellectual capital of a school (and its flows) must be rooted in the school's strategy. Indicators must bear a strong relation to the everyday operations of the school and should be prioritised into a weighted index, according to their importance to strategy. They should be relatively few in number, yet capture the essence of what each employee does. The inclination to try to capture everything in one super-indicator should be resisted, as should the inclination to adopt a different indicator for every trivial aspect of organisational life. Indicators should be sensitive, but not overly so; accurate insofar as they are able to differentiate between degrees of change; and reliable in that they actually measure what they purport to measure.

Schools committed to managing intellectual capital are learning organisations where employees learn how to learn, rather than learn what they need to know. What distinguishes leadership in learning organisations is metanoia and what distinguishes the organisation itself is the bias for action that sustains the impetus for change. For teachers, that means developing a collaborative culture that converts tacit knowledge to explicit knowledge; for headteachers, it means embracing the uncertainty and conflict that is endemic in schools. Layers of middle management are barriers to success in this respect, especially if they exist only to buffer leadership from the unpleasantness of decision making.

Schools can develop expertise organically through internal staff development, or by importing it through targeted recruitment. The latter approach is the one favoured by government for failing schools because it is immediate, though the extent to which the schools and their staffs benefit from it in the long-term is less certain; much depends on the accuracy of the assessment of their perceived needs and the extent to which the recruits possess matching skills. The former approach - internal staff development - is no less expensive though, involving as it does large numbers of staff over a protracted period of time. It is a commitment rather than an undertaking and much depends on the thoroughness of its design and the quality of its delivery.

The essential task of intellectual capital management is bringing people together in a deliberate manipulation to create capital from transfers of explicit and tacit knowledge. This can only be achieved through good communications. There should be formal structures for sharing knowledge, staff meetings should be organised efficiently, staff should be afforded structured opportunities for casual communication, there should be adequate common room facilities and junior teachers should be encouraged to the difficult task of sharing opinions and engaging in critical discussion with senior colleagues.

Measuring intellectual capital is largely a question of resource allocation. To make an accurate assessment of what is needed, there must first be an accurate assessment of what exists, so an audit of relevant tangible and intangible resources within the school should be made. While the immediate aim might be to measure how things are, the medium-term aim is to make things better, and this usually requires a shift in emphasis as far as incentivisation is concerned. There should be linkage between desired organisational outcomes and promotion criteria. Management must be prepared to focus incentives in such a way as to drive the organisation in the desired direction in an efficient manner.

Intellectual capital is not knowledge, but it is knowledge-based. It comes from an organisation's interaction with its environment and takes time to build. It is subjective and it increases in value with use. Schools should report regularly on the development of intellectual capital: reputation in the community, staff flexibility, acquired competencies such as the management of parent-teacher, teacher-pupil and community relations, experiential links with outside agencies such as examination boards, and so on. These are all dimensions to value creation and form a legitimate part of the story schools must tell stakeholders and by which they should ultimately be judged.

CHAPTER 2

Constructing a typology for intellectual capital

> Watch out for the fellow who talks about putting things in order! Putting things in order always means getting other people under your control.
>
> *Denis Diderot (1713 - 1784), 'Supplement to Bougainville's Voyage'.*

INTRODUCTION

It will be obvious from the discussion in the previous chapter that the flows of knowledge from one form of intellectual capital to another are critical and must be understood if benefits are to accrue to the organisation. So it is necessary to construct a typology of forms so that flows between forms can be mapped. Such a typology should allow managers to distinguish between different forms of intellectual capital and enable them to manage it at an operational level. In addition, the links between strategy and intellectual capital indicators (i.e. units of measurement) should be apparent so that the typology has *recognisability*; in other words, that it makes sense to both managers of strategy and managers of operations.

The most basic distinction to be made in constructing a typology of value-creating capital for schools - indeed for any organisation - is that between *hard asset capital* and *intangible asset capital* (see Figure 6). Hard asset or *financial* capital – the replacement value of an organisation - can be subdivided into *fixed* hard asset capital such as plant, machinery and equipment, and *liquid* hard asset capital, such as monetary reserves and borrowing facilities. The science of management of hard asset capital is well developed and needs no further exposition here; the management of intangible asset capital, on the other hand, is what this book is all about. It is intellectual capital in its broadest form and consists of all the processes and intangibles of a school. It can be sub-divided into *human* (to include *teacher / manager* and *student*) capital and *structural* capital.

In traditional commercial organisations, the human side of intellectual capital consists only of employees; customers are incorporated into the structural side because they are extrinsic to the organisation. That distinction is too crude for schools because of the intrinsic importance of the student voice in educational research and practice-led development (Fielding, 2001). Thus, in the typology represented in Figure 6, intellectual capital is primarily sub-categorised into *teacher / manager, student* and *structural* capitals. Teacher capital and student capital are *thinking* capitals; structural capital is not.

Categorising the contribution of parents to the intellectual capital of schools is more problematic.[10] It could justifiably be put into a category of its own, but is probably better accommodated under 'structural' because of its largely external focus.

The *structural* capital of a school can be thought of simply as the intangible assets of the school that remain when staff and students have gone home. It is the value that is added to a school by the organisation itself. It is not about the physical environment of the institution, but rather:

- The organisational structure that facilitates internal relationships, such as those between teachers, and between teachers and students. It includes the *organisational memory* of the school; that is, the codified modus operandi of the school and its personnel.
- The organisational structure that facilitates external relationships, such as those between the school and the community, and includes the non-financial contribution made by parents.

  It also incorporates less obvious things like the school's reputation in the community. For example, some of England's leading private schools – Shrewsbury, Harrow and Dulwich College – have franchised their brands (names, coats of arms, traditions, perceived expertise, and so on) in south-east Asia in return for a percentage of tuition fees.[11]
- The organisational structure of the school that facilitates innovation, adaptation and change, and more prosaically, staff development.

---

[10] In some circumstances, such as exist with pupils under the school-leaving age, the parent can be conceptualised as the customer. In other circumstances, such as with post-compulsory students, the parent is more peripheral to decision making; the student is the customer. It is subtle differences like this that make the analogy between commercial organisations and schools difficult to pursue, but instructive nevertheless.

[11] These schools have set up their 'international' namesakes in Thailand, which has no colonial connection with England, proving that the reputation being branded and sold is not just some sentimental relic of empire, but a genuine franchise extension.

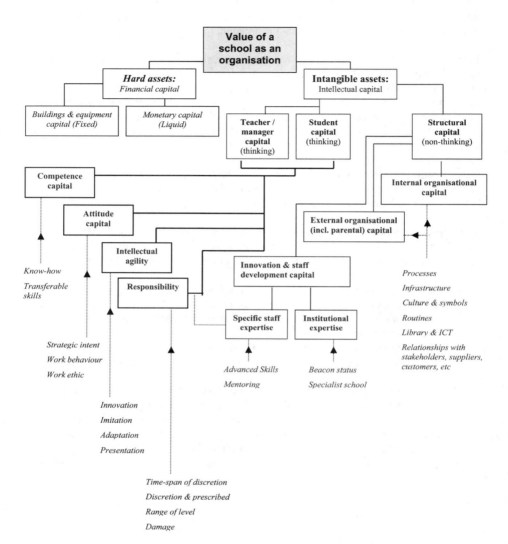

Figure 6. A typology of intellectual capitals

The structural or *non-thinking* capital of a school can be sub-categorised into *internal organisational* capital, *external organisational* capital and *innovation and staff development* capital. Both forms of organisational capital, internal and external, consist largely of *process* capital. Process capital is the codified experience and routines of those who work in the school: development manuals, library and ICT resources, relationships with stakeholders, suppliers and examination boards, and so on. The third form of structural capital, innovation and staff development capital, is what creates future success. It represents the ability of the organisation to renew itself. It consists of both institutional expertise, such as beacon and special school status, and individual teacher expertise, which includes advanced teaching skills, experience mentoring newly qualified teachers, and so on.

Teacher / manager and student capitals, being forms of thinking capital, require a different managerial approach to that of structural capital, which is non-thinking. Managers, teachers[12] and students generate capital for a school through their competence, their attitude, their intellectual agility and through their endeavours to increase their levels of responsibility. Headteachers generally recognise the importance of student capital, apart from any involvement students may have in organisational development and research: some yearly intakes are good, others are not so good, and the perceived worth of a school rises or falls on their achievement and behaviour over the course of their stay.

Thinking capital can best be understood in terms of its constituent parts:
- *Competence capital* is the general sum of skills, both generic and transferable, and knowledge.
- *Attitude capital* is the behavioural component of work. It comprises motivation, work ethic and the like.
- *Intellectual agility* is the ability of teachers, managers and students to innovate and change practice, to think 'outside the box' about problems and come up with novel solutions. Intellectual agility is neither a competence nor an attitude, but a mixture of both. Its components include imitation, innovation, adaptation and presentation.
- The *responsibility of a job* can be measured in terms of its *discretionary element*, its *time-span of discretion* and its *range of level of work*. These are all considered in detail in the next chapter.

Knowledge, both tacit and explicit, is the primary source of intellectual capital, though it has been sub-categorised above as teacher / manager, student and structural. While teacher / manager and student capitals are obviously linked by virtue of the fact that they are both forms of thinking capital, there are also links between these

---

[12] The term includes teaching assistants, trainee-teachers, and so on.

thinking capitals and structural capital, which is non-thinking. These links become
more apparent as the sources of supply for each are considered in greater detail.

THINKING CAPITAL

The intellectual capital value of a school, like the share value of a commercial
company, is predicated on its key personnel. When highly esteemed individuals leave,
the stock falls; when new ones arrive, the stock rises. For schools, this at once
demonstrates both the importance of thinking capital in the shape of managers,
teachers and students, and the somewhat despairing fact for headteachers that most of
a school's value is beyond their control, because a school cannot retain or dispose of
its own thinking capital as and when it pleases. Student capital and teacher / manager
capital rest on slightly different footings here. Retention and disposal of student
capital is completely beyond a school manager's control in one respect, but easily
managed in another. While a school cannot reasonably detain or dispose of students
against their will, it does have what might be called *predictive control* over the length
of their stay, which can be determined typically within a five-to-seven year period. On
the other hand, teachers and managers leave at times of their own choosing; in fact,
the more essential they are, the more likely is their move in many ways.[13]
It is relatively difficult for not-for-profit organisations like schools to retain key
personnel using incentives. In public (state) schools, there is no facility for profit-
sharing schemes since there is no profit; and in private (fee-paying) schools, which
can offer fee-reduction schemes for children of staff and such like, the retention effect
is reduced by the fact that all such schools offer more or less the same package.
Additionally, in commercial organisations, profit sharing and share option incentives
allow profits to remain available for re-investment by the company in the short-to-
medium term, since there is no immediate likelihood of drawdown. This is a different
situation from the one that obtains in (private) schools, where school fee remission is
more reasonably regarded simply as a loss of income, because although there is often
no immediate prospect of drawdown, there is nothing for the organisation to reinvest.
Nevertheless, school fee remission is an effective retention incentive in the private
school sector, and some thought could usefully be given to how state sector schools
might do something similar; in other words, incentivise teacher recruitment and
retention through surrogates like income tax concessions, mortgage relief on
accommodation, and so on. Replacing and training staff places a heavy financial
burden on any system and additionally gives rise to instability and poor planning.
State schools in particular have a pressing need to develop a comprehensive
incentivisation strategy for the retention of staff.

Competence capital
Competence capital generates value through individual and collective know-how.
Know-how is a combination of technical knowledge, managerial and human relations
skill, and problem-solving ability. It is the hard part of thinking capital.

---

[13] This is more noticeable in private (fee-paying) schools, where heads of boarding houses typically
move to new schools every few years and headteachers usually have a pastoral background as opposed
to a curriculum background. (The opposite is the case in the state sector).

- In schools, *technical knowledge* ranges from simple familiarity with school routines to externally recognised expertise and professional eminence in the field of education.
- *Managerial and human relations skills* range from doing or directing routine activities to managing disparate groups of varied jobs.
- *Human relations skills* range from the basic ability to deal courteously with colleagues to motivating, understanding and influencing reluctant colleagues and outsiders to act in the interest of the school rather than themselves.
- *Problem solving* is the extent to which know-how is required to solve a job's problems. Since people think with what they know, problem solving can be regarded as a subset of know-how.

Competence is generally related to level of education. It has to be taught, but not necessarily in teacher-training colleges or universities. It cannot be acquired by trial-and-error, but requires formal instruction.

Technical or academic knowledge, as a constituent of competence capital, is not embedded in an organisation. Embedded capital is structural and can only be explicit, whereas technical / academic knowledge is neither.

If knowledge is a theoretical consideration, skill is its practical counterpart. Skill is the practical application of knowledge, and the most useful skills are the ones that are generic and transferable. Skills cannot be transmitted by formal instruction, only through the practicum of experience, but they are relatively easy to communicate because they can be codified and shared within an organisation or between organisations. Skills are only distantly related to knowledge, although they usually increase and decrease in line with each other. A person with a high level of technical knowledge can have a low level of practical skill, and vice versa. For example, most people have the skill to operate a television set, but few have the technical knowledge that comes with knowing how it works or the academic knowledge of knowing why.

Attitude capital

Merely having know-how and competence is not sufficient to guarantee success. Employees must be capable and motivated to use their competence capital to the advantage of the school, and not just themselves. If competence is the hard component of thinking capital, attitude is its soft counterpart. Organisations can do little to manage attitude capital. It depends mostly on individual personality traits and there is not much that can be done by managers to improve it across an organisation. At best, all they can do is create a supportive work environment, or hire people with the 'right' attitude and develop know-how later, in-house, which is what generally happens in the commercial sector.

Strategic intent, work behaviour and work ethic are among the significant contributors to attitude capital. *Strategic intent* (Hamel & Prahalad, 1989) is the willingness to persevere in pursuit of organisational goals, and the desire and ability to imagine a future, convince others to work towards it and eventually create it. It implies an ability to refine and redefine strategies, to learn quickly from failure and to manage change. It is largely an amalgam of motivation and vision.

Work behaviour leads to enhanced productivity if it helps create a dynamic work environment and enthuses others. Work behaviour that serves this end should be encouraged and other behaviours discouraged. Good work behaviour must be sustained and consistent over a period of time for it to be of long-term benefit to a school. It needs to encourage contact and generate activity - the term *contactivity* best describes it – which in turn liberates employee enthusiasm and harnesses it to create a better shared future. Many commercial companies - British Telecom and Skandia being two examples – consciously enable disparate individuals within the company to come together and share their aspirations, interpretations and extrapolations, sometimes with the help of futurologists.[14]

Whereas work behaviour is essentially strategic in outlook, *work ethic* is judgemental. It judges behaviour not from the standpoint of future success, but from the point of view of the existing ethical values of the society in which the school is operating. It is by definition value-laden and depends on external societal judgements, so a school has little control over it. It is not so much an important source of capital as an important *drain* on capital when it is absent, as evidenced by the bad publicity generated by commercial companies who are deemed (by the court of public opinion) to have behaved reprehensibly. Consumer power – some would say consumer *responsibility* - is such nowadays that unethical or environment-unfriendly behaviour leads very quickly to a boycott of goods or services and the effect on a company's bottom line is not insignificant.

Intellectual agility capital

Intellectual agility is the ability to jump knowledge between contexts and between situations, and to innovate and transform ideas critical to the success of a school. It relies on an ability to detect commonalities in distinct pieces of information and piece them together in an original way. It is at the core of innovation and adaptation, and in a commercial environment, diversification.[15] Intellectual agility depends on the ability to apply competence to practical situations and to learn from failure. It is the normative side of knowledge and its constituents include innovation capital, imitation capital, adaptation capital and presentation capital.

Innovation capital is the specific ability to generate new knowledge by building on experience and by absorbing an existing body of know-how and adding to it. In the commercial world, it is the ability to turn an idea into a product and represents a link between human and structural capital. It is fundamental to the ability to generate renewal and manage change, which aspects in turn are necessary for sustaining success.

An increase in the store of innovation capital may come in an evolutionary way (incremental change) from codifying subsequent insights in the light of experience, or in a revolutionary way (step change) through a fundamental reassessment of operational processes. In for-profit organisations, particularly high-tech and pharmaceutical ones, innovation comes about through research and development, which is formally and explicitly catered for in the structure of the company itself. On the other hand, not-for-profit organisations like schools typically innovate as a result of outside imposition, which is tacitly catered for by the mechanisms that make them accountable to society, such as school inspection systems.

---

[14] British Telecom, for example, employs a Futurologist at its research facilities near Ipswich, UK.

[15] Richard Branson's Virgin Group, for example, has achieved its success through jumping its specialist knowledge of the youth market to many diverse industries; airlines, music, insurance, travel and on-line banking.

Imitation capital is the opportunity and ability to replicate in one's own organisation the good practice taking place in another, and to adapt and sometimes improve upon it. As Roos et al (1997) point out, imitation sometimes has negative connotations because it suggests an inability to invent for oneself. However, in more general terms, this is unfair; not everything that comes out of imitation is inferior. Imitation usually leads in the longer term to something new[16] or something better, and gives rise to organisational structures that facilitate the cross fertilisation of ideas, such as exist in collegial universities like Oxford and Cambridge. The boundaries between innovation and imitation are ill-defined, but both can be sources of significant improvement.

In the commercial sector, *adaptation capital* comes about as a result of changes in the competitive environment, in the dominant technology, in government regulation, in the nature of the market and in consumer demand. Adaptation capital is *reactive* if the organisation is compelled to change by circumstance or imposition; *anticipative* if the organisation is voluntarily adapting to take account of forecasted changes; and *creative* if it is trying to manufacture its own future by imposing itself or its new product on a market. Creative adaptation offers the greatest opportunity for staff to share ownership of change - something which Fullan (1991) and others tell us is necessary for long-term organisational improvement - but it is the one least commonly seen in education. For some time now, schools and teachers have not been trusted with creating their own futures and as a consequence, organisational systems for developing creative capital are weak in schools. Creative capital both demands and creates strong systems. Its absence results in a loss in motivation for staff.

Presentation capital is about generating enthusiasm among customers for a product or service. It is about creating a need or the perception of a need and is a link between human and monetary capital. In schools, it is about communicating enthusiasm to staff, parents and pupils for curriculum innovation, for changes in working practices, for raising expectations and how these can result in better educational outcomes.

Responsibility
The responsibility of a job – the set of recognisable, recurring, non-exceptional duties and responsibilities undertaken by an employee - can be measured in terms of its time-span of discretion, its range of level of work and its discretionary and prescribed elements. The measurement of responsibility and the evaluation of jobs using guide-charts are described in greater detail in the next chapter, but central to the idea of both is the question of determining appropriate remuneration and status for individuals, an emotive issue since it questions an employee's security, value and perceived usefulness to others.

The *time-span of discretion* of a job is the period of time that elapses before the effects of an employee's discretion become apparent to a manager. The maximum time-span of discretion for any given job is a measure of the value of the job to the organisation.

---

[16] The Japanese language is one example; the written form was imported from Chinese and the grammar from Korean.

Range of level of work is defined as the widest range within which work can be allocated to an incumbent, from the lowest level compatible with the work being done to the highest level available to be assigned. *Level of work* is a measure of the intensity of responsibility in a job. It is not equivalent to *quantity of work*, which is the amount of work done irrespective of level of responsibility, but it is the aspect of a job that should merit differentiation in status or pay. Too often, pay and status is related to quantity, rather than level, of work.

The *discretionary content* of a job consists of those elements about which an employee has freedom of choice; in other words, those elements for which the work itself does not automatically determine the best method of doing it. The *prescribed content* of a job, on the other hand, consists of those elements about which the employee has *no* choice. The target is set by a manager and / or limits are set on the employee by the means available to do the work. Clearly, it is the discretionary part of a job that should determine remuneration and status, or more precisely, differentiation in remuneration and status.

Research suggests that employees attach considerable importance to the amount of work rejected as not being up to standard, or *scrappage* as it has been called (Jaques, 1956).[17] It is a concept allied to that of discretionary content. The amount of scrappage that an organisation relies on employees to avoid through the use of their own discretion - *damage avoidance* - gives a measure of the amount of responsibility carried by a job. Jobs that carry greater amounts of damage avoidance are ones that employees themselves consider should receive higher rates. The concept can be adapted to a school setting as *interference avoidance*. It is discussed in detail in the following chapter. In schools, there is an acceptance that jobs with greater discretion carry greater expectations of interference avoidance; they are allowed less inadvertent interference with the normal functioning of the school and are expected to carry a broader whole-school view of things as a consequence.

NON-THINKING CAPITAL

The non-thinking component of intellectual capital is structural capital, which consists of all the value-adding institutional processes, routines and infrastructures that remain in the school when students, teachers and staff have gone home. In includes:

- ICT and library resources.
- Codified expertise, both collective and individual, and advanced teaching and mentoring skills.
- Relationships built over time with students and parents, between teachers, between managers and governors, and with suppliers, examination boards and local community groups.
- Databases, organisational charts, and mentoring and training manuals.
- Intellectual property rights such as textbook authorships (and in the case of commercial companies, patents).
- Organisational culture and ethos (Hargreaves, 1967; Dalin, 1993).

---

[17] Jaques coined the term for workers in an industrial setting, but we extend it here for use in any sector.

Structural (non-thinking) capital is possessed by an organisation, whereas human (thinking) capital is not. Mailing lists, student and parent databases, innovations, authorships and resources are all obviously owned by an organisation, but since these sources of structural capital are not possessed by any one person or group, their development is slower and their management more difficult than is the case with human capital. Human capital is increased just by people living their lives. Structural capital, on the other hand, needs to be proactively updated by employees themselves. It is proprietary, but not self-renewing.

Three distinct components of structural capital can be identified: external organisational capital, internal organisational capital, and innovation and staff development capital.

External organisational capital

External organisational capital is the external component of structural capital. In education, as in the commercial sector, markets have become increasingly interconnected and there is a corresponding need to rely on external factors for the successful everyday operation of an organisation. In schools, external organisational capital largely consists of value generated by parents, although they lie on the boundary between internal and external stakeholding.

A school's relationship with its parent body is continuous. It does not comprise sets of discrete yearly or rolling five-yearly cohorts, as is sometimes thought. Individual parents talk to one another. They are part of a wider community that includes parents of former and prospective students. Last year's parent cohort cannot be separated from future cohorts and good relationships with parents are only built up over time. Likewise with suppliers, local education authorities, the schools inspectorate, examination boards, community groups and alumni. And it is precisely because of the increasing importance of these relationships with external stakeholders that schools need to take a long-term view of intellectual capital.

At the core of this extended notion of external organisational capital is *customer loyalty*. It is difficult to put a value on it, even in a commercial company, though everyone recognises its importance: generations of a family bank with the same company however cost-ineffective it might be; shoppers continue to shop with certain retailers for no good reason; travellers fly with the same airline out of habit. Some of this inertia, though not all, can be put down to a natural reluctance to engage with the difficulties associated with change. It is bothersome to change banks, to transfer debt, to cancel standing orders and so on, but the same cannot be said for changing airlines or cash-shopping, where it is as easy to change as not to change.

Commercial companies have long recognised the bottom-line value of loyalty, a fact evidenced by the proliferation of store loyalty cards, credit cards that offer cash-back at the end of every year, and frequent flier air-mile schemes. Enthusiasm among companies for recruiting customers from competitors, while locking in their own, knows few bounds.[18] Customer satisfaction, apart from enhancing the reputation of an organisation, increases the life expectancy of its external capital and makes it easier to attract new clients (Fornell, 1992). Recruiting new customers is more costly and more painful than retaining existing ones, so any organisation with an eye to the future must pay heed to the satisfaction of its existing customers.

---

[18] This is something that has been causing concern in the United Kingdom among regulators of gas and electricity suppliers, and consumer organisations have called for statutory regulation to replace the voluntary code of practice and to curb overly aggressive sales tactics.

A loyal customer base can also be exploited for the purposes of brand extension. Long-term consumers naturally tend to trust a company with which they have a long-standing relationship, and they are consequently more inclined to try new products when they come to the market.

It is more difficult to put a value on the extent to which a school has loyal 'customers', how well it is regarded in the local community and the extent to which it has long-term satisfactory relationships with key external agencies like examination boards. At least in commercial organisations, the efficacy or otherwise of loyalty can be fairly judged in terms of market share, turnover and profit at the end of the trading year. For schools, recruitment of pupils from the local catchment area might seem an obvious surrogate, but it is not a good measure on its own because parents often have no choice. There can be no customer loyalty without freedom of choice. As long as schools recruit only from prescribed catchments and as long as those within catchments are forced to attend only designated schools, there can be no real measure of customer loyalty in education. That is unfortunate because brand extension is something schools do all the time; they ask parents to trust them when it comes to curriculum change, when it comes to changing from one examining board to another, when it comes to Sixth Form choices and university entrance, when they say that an overseas trip will be educationally beneficial, when a sister school is set up at home or overseas, and so on.[19]

In the commercial sector, external agencies and suppliers are now considered an integral part of the organisation of a company. In some situations, suppliers even have a physical presence within client organisations, to reduce marketing, travel and training costs. It is a symbiotic relationship, enhancing the value of both client and supplier organisations, and encouraging closer relationships. As a consequence, competition is nowadays often between strategic *client-supplier chains*, rather than between individual suppliers or between individual companies.

Strategic alliances have become increasingly important, especially in competitive deregulated sectors such as commercial aviation.[20] For example, the One World alliance (British Airways, Qantas, United Airlines and others) battles the Star alliance (Luftansa, Austrian Airways, Air Canada and others) for market dominance. The competition is between alliances, not between airlines. And new alliances form on the high street with increasing frequency, such as that in the UK between British Petroleum, Sainsbury, Barclays and Debenhams through the 'Nectar Card' chain.

Strategic alliances are possible in the education world too. The obvious ones are between schools, and between schools, further education colleges and universities. Less obvious – certainly less common – are the possible alliances between schools and awarding bodies, between headteacher and curriculum associations, between awarding bodies and teacher unions, and so on. It is mostly unexplored terrain, but it is one ripe for exploitation.

Choosing the right partners for an alliance is critical and the ability to select a complementary partner is a key managerial competence. Synergy is the watchword and more efficient access to bigger markets the objective. Every alliance is looking to rationalise the service it offers customers. For example, British Airways and Aer

---

[19] See also Footnote 11.

[20] Competitiveness in the commercial aviation sector can be traced to the deregulation of the US market (led by Professor Alfred Kahn of Cornell University, chairman then of the Civil Aeronautics Board) during the Carter administration.

Lingus, the two national carriers on the Dublin to London route,[21] are joined together in the One World syndicate for both ticketing and travel, in a combined effort to ward off the challenge from low-cost, no-frills competitors like Ryanair. Gone are the days, it appears, when governments threatened trade wars over the landing rights enjoyed (or not) by flag carriers in each other's jurisdictions.

Alliances vary in the extent of their formality. They range from long-term, legally binding, joint ventures to ad hoc customer-supplier friendships, although that dichotomy is blurred when de facto oligopolies exist between competitors.[22] But even in formal synergistic strategic alliances, success depends on good customer relations. These are underpinned in commercial companies by the fact that strategic decisions must ultimately be approved by shareholders, and in schools by the fact that policy actions are subject to approval annually by governing bodies. Shareholders and stakeholders are customers too, and they are sometimes aware of their power and sometimes not. Having an internal legal function in addition to being a customer (like parent governors in schools, for instance) means that organisations can be guided to the correct action in the marketplace by the market itself.[23] It is nearly always a good thing. Good customer relations are a necessity, not a luxury.

Relationship capital, especially that from external stakeholders, can be a powerful weapon in a school's struggle to achieve its strategic objectives. Conveniently, it replenishes and renews itself. Existing relationships beget new relationships without any active effort on the part of teachers or managers necessarily. Parents have an obvious role to play. They support the school's efforts in terms of supplying pupils, helping with homework, fundraising, acting as unpaid assistants and generally providing the liaison between school and home that school effectiveness research suggests is a prerequisite to educational success (Levine & Lezotte, 1990; Rowe, Hill & Holmes-Smith, 1994).

The nature of parental involvement is critical. There are positive effects to parents helping in the classroom and such like, but negative effects (or none) from run-of-the-mill involvement in parents' associations and extracurricular activities (Mortimore et al., 1988; Sammons, Hillman & Mortimore, 1995). Destructive parental involvement, which frequently manifests itself in aggressive behaviour towards teachers, unfair public criticism and unreasonable expectations, most often occurs in schools serving low socio-economic areas (Teddlie & Stringfield, 1993), but wherever it occurs it generates ineffectiveness, and one of the (exhausting) functions of headship in such circumstances is to buffer the school community from it.

Research suggests that parents themselves feel that there are important benefits to be had from close cooperation between home and school, which include having a better understanding of school and examination processes, being reassured about student progress or lack of it, and finding out how best to support the school as it tackles sensitive issues. Parents typically regard a healthy home-school relationship as one

---

[21] The busiest air route in Europe.

[22] In the UK education sector, for example, a triopoly could be said to exist between the three unitary awarding bodies; Edexcel, AQA and OCR. They have large tracts of school and college territory divided up between them - in fact, if not by agreement - and they are engaged in what is effectively a long-term triple alliance.

[23] Stakeholder actions can greatly influence the operations of public companies, as evidenced by the popular agitation against Shell petrol in 1995 over the company's decision to sink the disused Brent Spar oilrig at sea.

where a friendly atmosphere exists between teachers and parents, where caring teachers communicate well with pupils, where discipline is firm but fair, where there is good monitoring of pupil progress, and where there is an active and supportive parent body (MacBeath, 1999).

Internal organisational capital

Internal organisational capital is proprietary, but unlike external relationship capital, is not self-replenishing. It needs pro-activity on the part of management and the day-to-day support of teachers to survive. Internal organisational capital comprises all the non-thinking capital related to the internal structure and day-to-day operation of a school. Sources include student databases, mentoring guidelines, teaching manuals, and intangibles such as ethos and style of management. Internal organisational capital is usually the result of effort on the part of the organisation to turn human capital into explicit knowledge, and to share that knowledge among all its employees and stakeholders. Internal networks and intranets are therefore part of this category.

Apart from the contribution of relationships to general organisational capital, already discussed above, there are three main constituent aspects to internal organisational capital: *infrastructure* capital (including organisational routines); *process and resource* capital; *culture* capital.

Infrastructure capital is the sum value coming from the structure of an organisation and its intellectual property assets; patents, trademarks, publications, brands, and so on. Infrastructure represents the hardware part of a company. It must be flexible enough to grow in parallel with the organic growth of its employees, but bureaucratic enough to offer them security and predictability. It must be capable of connecting employees to each other at all levels of the organisation, and it must facilitate information sharing between employees and between parts of the organisation. The most successful aspects of it should be reproducible and in that sense, the systems of the organisation should have *memory*.

Intellectual property is an increasingly important part of infrastructure capital. It traditionally comprises patents and copyright, but can include things like mailing lists, customer, student and alumni databases, and process, mentoring and training manuals, which are all nowadays granted similar measures of legal protection.

If the infrastructure of a company is its hardware, *process capital* is its operational software. It is what makes an organisation tick. Having a good infrastructure is a necessary but not sufficient condition for success. The structure has to operate properly and employees must know how to use it to achieve the organisation's aims. Process capital can be passed from colleague to colleague by word of mouth or through documentation. The latter is preferable because it guarantees that the organisation has explicit memory of its own procedures. All internal activities are processes and they contribute to the organisation's internal capital as long as they are shared among employees. So the critical competence for managers is to take all the various processes, procedures and interactions, and plan strategically for the knowledge that is extracted from them to be shared. Initially, this is likely to be a matter of trial and error, but over time, managers should be able to build databases of best practice for replication across the organisation. This is the essence of knowledge management. Some commercial companies have even gone so far as to create a position of *Learning Controller*, whose task it is to ensure that process capital is thus transformed into infrastructure capital.

The third constituent of internal organisational capital is *cultural capital*. It is the soft, evolving part: a series of rights, symbols and norms that define an organisation every bit as much as its physical counterpart. Ethos is surface lying. It is the outward expression of culture; how the organisation feels to visitors, its friendliness, the helpfulness of its staff and so on. Culture, on the other hand, lies deeper. It is the organisation's underpinning system of beliefs and attitudes, its way of doing and its historical inheritance. Culture is created by the constant interaction of employees and stakeholders, and the more substantial these interactions, the stronger the culture. If employees do not interact, no organisational culture can be created. It is simultaneously a cognitive activity and a metaphorical creation, the sum of all the individual biographies of the people who have a stake in the school.

Culture is important in providing staff with a framework within which to interpret events. It helps stakeholders to select only relevant events from the myriad that constitutes the daily pattern of life in a modern school, avoiding sensory overload. It influences management style and creates a social norm for managers to follow while simultaneously motivating employees to strive for organisational rather than selfish goals.

Symbolism has an important influence on culture, especially school culture. It affirms a school's own vision of itself; a mix of recognition and history used to influence the perception and sense-making activities of teachers, pupils and others. It originates in the school's ability to craft a vision of reality powerful enough to be accepted by stakeholders and competitors alike, but its value is greatest with respect to internal relationships.

Effective schools have a culture in which academic emulation is encouraged (McDill & Rigsby, 1973), though research suggests that schools have many cultures expressing themselves at different levels, rather than one single culture (MacBeath, 1999; MacBeath & McGlynn, 2002). Dalin and Rust (1996) similarly describe culture as operating on as many as three different levels, sometimes at the same time: the *transrational level*, where a sense of mission is promulgated on moral and ethical values; the *rational level*, where stakeholders accept institutional routines and customs because they make sense; the *sub-rational level*, where norms derive from personal preference and are grounded in subjective experience. But no matter how complex is the theoretical model of school culture, there is always value in investigating it as part of intellectual capital management because it has the power to confront an organisation with its own value system and provide an opportunity – especially important in schools - to challenge rituals that may have become embedded over time but which have ceased to serve any useful purpose (MacBeath & McGlynn, 2002).

Innovation and staff development capital

The last category of structural capital is *innovation and development* capital. It comprises the intangible side of anything that has the potential to generate value in the future but does not yet have an impact. Planning for investment and renewal in buildings and equipment is part of innovation and development capital, though it becomes *fixed hard asset capital* when it is built or installed. Similarly, investment in training employees is staff development capital as far as planning is concerned; after the training takes place, it becomes human capital. Curriculum development, restructuring procedures, the development of new mentoring schemes and teacher in-service programmes are all examples of innovation and development capital.

In some ways, innovation and development capital represents a conceptualisation of the inevitable time delay between planning and implementation, between inception and realisation. The challenge for managers is to balance the need for future investment with the need for immediate organisational prosperity, something that is particularly true for schools in terms of examination success. Management must strive to create and maintain a renewal strategy that is consistent with both the immediate needs of the organisation and the longer-term goals the organisation has set itself.

FLOWS OF INTELLECTUAL CAPITAL

The flows of intellectual capital from one form to another can be mapped over the typology of intellectual capital described above. It would be impossible to manage it otherwise. It can never be enough to manage intellectual capital like an inventory of spare parts, merely recording increases and decreases on a balance sheet. Managers need to understand why some intellectual capital stocks rise and others fall, and they need to understand why certain mechanisms for remediation and compensation work while others do not, and under what circumstances. The objective is plain enough - to monitor and manage the intangible assets of the school in an efficient manner - but there are difficulties.

The time-delay problem

Flows of intellectual capital usually involve significant but unpredictable time delays. In the education sector, these depend on the particular school, its stage of organisational maturity and the nature of its catchment area. Forecasting is extremely difficult. For example, it takes time – an unknowable length of time – for teacher in-service training to affect practice, if it does at all. Teachers need time to assimilate change, to reflect upon it and to justify it professionally by incorporating it into their own practice. They may wait for the right occasion to put new ideas into practice and this may not occur for some time. This creates difficulties for managers in relation to auditing intellectual capital and difficulties for the teachers themselves in that the newly acquired skill might be outmoded by the time it is actually used.

On a more hopeful note, the very act of increasing staff competence, whether or not it is fully incorporated into practice, can kick-start a cycle of improvement and professional reflection that can only be beneficial. It is important to remember that a culture of improvement is spread by imitation and social interaction, not by managerial dictat, so what might seem to an anxious headteacher like a waste of money can be very profitable in the longer term. This is not to underestimate the difficulty of having these *sleeper flows*; they do create havoc with measurement systems. The trick is to decide which flows are going to result in increases in intellectual capital and which ones are going to fizzle out.

The zero-sum problem

Intellectual capital is not a zero-sum game. Financial investment in buildings, equipment and training can be very large, yet fail to convert itself into an appreciable asset. Some investments have lower leverage than others. Unlike flows from financial to financial capital, intellectual capital flows don't add up. It is not the case that what is lost or used in one form of intellectual capital, is created in another. There is no law of conservation of intellectual capital as it changes form, which is why it cannot be managed like an inventory.

The measurement by proxy problem

There is a difficulty with units of measurement for intellectual capital. Traditional financial stocks are measured in units of national currency obviously, but intellectual capital indicators do not enjoy such standardisation. Instead they use a mixture of *numeric proxies* to give an idea of size and flow; Likert scale ratings, man-hours worked, assessments of competence, and the like. This situation creates a difficulty when comparisons between organisations or between disparate groups within an organisation are made, but as long as the proxies are used consistently, it is largely a question of being aware of the potential pitfalls.

	Competence Capital	Attitude capital	Intellectual agility capital	Relationship capital	Organisational capital	Innovation & development capital	Financial capital
Competence capital	Reflection on INSET courses, theories of teaching & learning, training etc.	Increasing drive to learn from the environment & from interactions	Leading to cross fertilisation of ideas; research & development	Leading to exchange of ideas & development of skills; reflection on assumptions	Encouraging learning & reflective practice; codification of reflection	Better research, development & training	Training teachers and hiring key people
Attitude capital	Maturing effect; confidence boosting	Reinforcing good practice among teachers	Learning new behaviour	Generating goodwill & optimism among stakeholders	Creating cultural legends as a means of showing the desired attitude	Demanding & generating new behaviours	NONE
Intellectual agility capital	Stimulation to develop (and expect to develop) new skills	Driving innovation	Sharpening of intellectual agility through repetition	Driving the need to develop relationships for growth	Develops team spirit, but beware the 'yes' culture	Driving the search for new ways of innovating, adapting & imitating	Creating the ability to see different solutions
Relationship capital	Leading to assessment of synergies in organisational relationships	Setting goals for the partnerships	Developing new ways to link with partners; & searching for new partners	Developing relationships through social interaction, but beware halo & demon effects	Building relationships into the infrastructural memory	Driving the search for new relations	Funding relationships and partnerships; looking for value for money
Organisational capital	Creating of new structures & thinking outside the box	Leading from the front; the head as exemplary practitioner	Structural & cultural innovation	Developing new organisational forms through relationships	Modifying and reinforcing what works	Developing new structures & processes	Funding organisational & cultural change events
Innovation & development capital	Discovering & exploring	Driving renewal	Driving creativity and innovation	Driving the search for new alternatives	Shifting the cultural orientation of the school towards the future	Encouraging innovative staff development	Investing in the future development of the school and its staff
Financial capital	Adding value in teacher expertise and beacon-type status	Funding to reinforce the desired attitude	Developing intellectual property; cost savings through in-house innovation	Increasing stakeholder satisfaction and enhancing reputation of the school	Cost savings through re-structuring	Developing new curriculum approaches	Traditional balance sheet accounting

Figure 7. The confluences of intellectual capital flows: some examples

NEW LANGUAGE; NEW MEASURES

Figure 7 gives an overview of flows of intellectual capital from one form to another. It is necessary to understand these flows if measurement is to be undertaken, and there is a need to develop a common language for all stakeholders involved in that process. At the end of the day, information must be shared in order to generate further intellectual capital, and for it to be shared, it must have a common language.

It has been mentioned already that constructing an intellectual capital typology can help an organisation understand some hitherto unclear issues, the most important of which is the contribution that each individual employee makes to the organisation and the cost of that contribution in terms of the financial capital each employee is absorbing. And connections between different intellectual capital stocks can also become clearer. For example, the three-way relationship between a headteacher's practice, the school's progress towards an agreed goal and individual teacher motivation becomes clearer when viewed as a flow of capital from human to structural form, and back again. This will be dealt with in later chapters.

SUMMARY

A typology of forms of intellectual capital allows managers to manage flows of capital at an operational level. The most basic distinction to be made is that between hard asset capital and intangible asset capital. Intangible asset capital consists of all the processes and intangibles of a school, and is sub-divided into human (thinking) and structural (non-thinking) capital.

Human capital is best understood in terms of its constituent components: Competence capital - the general sum of skills and knowledge; Attitude capital - the behavioural component of work; Intellectual agility - the ability of teachers, managers and students to innovate and think outside the box; and Responsibility, which is measured in terms of its discretion, its time-span of discretion and its range of level of work.

- Competence capital generates value through know-how, which is a combination of technical knowledge, managerial skill, human relations skill and problem-solving ability: technical knowledge ranges from simple familiarity with school routines to externally recognised professional eminence; managerial and human relations skill ranges from directing routine activities to managing disparate groups of varied jobs; human relations skill ranges from the ability to deal courteously with colleagues to motivating, understanding and influencing reluctant colleagues and outsiders to act in the interest of the organisation; and problem-solving ability is the extent to which know-how is used to solve a job's problems.
- Having know-how is not enough to guarantee success. Teachers must be capable and motivated to use their competence capital to the advantage of the school and not themselves. If competence is the hard component of thinking

capital, attitude capital is its soft counterpart. Strategic intent, work behaviour and work ethic are among the significant factors that affect it.

- Intellectual agility is the ability to jump knowledge between contexts and between situations, and to innovate and transform ideas critical to the success of a school. Innovation, imitation, adaptation and presentation capitals are constituents: innovation capital is the specific ability to generate new knowledge by building on experience, by absorbing an existing body of know-how and adding to it; imitation capital is the opportunity and ability to replicate in one's own school the good practice taking place in another, and to improve upon it; adaptation capital is a measure of how a school responds to change; presentation capital is about generating enthusiasm among customers for a service by creating a need or the perception of a need.
- The responsibility of a job – the set of recognisable, recurring, non-exceptional duties and responsibilities undertaken by an employee - can be measured in terms of its time-span of discretion, its range of level of work and its discretionary and prescribed elements.

The structural capital of a school consists of the intangible assets of the organisation that remain when staff and students go home. It is the value that is added to the organisation by the organisation itself: the structure that facilitates organisational memory, external relationships, innovation, adaptation and change, and staff development. It can be sub-categorised into internal organisational capital, external organisational capital and innovation and staff development capital. Both internal and external organisational capitals consist largely of process capital, the codified experience and routines of those who work within the school. Innovation and staff development capital represents the ability of the school to renew itself.

Structural capital, unlike human capital, is possessed by an organisation, but because it is not possessed by any one person or group, its development is slower and its management more difficult than is the case with human capital. Human capital is increased just by people living their lives, whereas structural capital needs to be proactively updated by employees themselves. It is proprietary, but not self-renewing.

CHAPTER 3

The measurement of responsibility

> Whether a man is burdened by power or enjoys it; whether he is trapped by responsibility or made free by it; whether he is moved by other people and outer forces or moves them - this is of the essence of leadership.
>
> *Theodore H. White, 1906 - 1964.*

INTRODUCTION

A *job* can be defined as a set of recognisable, recurring, non-exceptional duties and responsibilities assigned to an *employee* or *incumbent*. These duties and responsibilities, discharged through *work*, are collectively the *functions* of the job and a *job description* is a public narrative statement of these functions. The term *job* is little used among salaried professionals who prefer euphemistic terms like *position* to imply something over and above what waged non-professionals do, but except for these subtle social distinctions, 'job' and 'position' have the same meaning.

A *job profile* is an extended, contextualised job description. It should include general information about the working environment and the management structure, and it should describe the skills and know-how required to do the job successfully.

Know-how is a form of competence capital. It is the sum of technical or scientific knowledge, managerial and human relations skill, and problem-solving ability.

- For schools, *technical knowledge* ranges from simple familiarity with school routines to externally recognised expertise and professional eminence in the field of education.
- *Managerial skill* ranges from doing or directing activities similar to each other to managing disparate groups of jobs with different and varied functions.

- *Human relations skill* ranges from normal courtesy in dealing with teaching colleagues to motivating, understanding and influencing reluctant stakeholders to act not in their own interest, but in the interest of the school.
- *Problem-solving* is the extent to which know-how is required by the incumbent to overcome the difficulties thrown up by the job. People think with what they know, so problem solving can be thought of as a simple percentage of know-how.

There is a distinction to be made between duties and responsibilities. *Responsibilities* are the activities that define a job; *duties* are activities done in pursuit of the responsibility. A *manager* is an employee who acts legally on behalf of an employer, and in the sense that managers have authority over *subordinates*, are of a higher rank within the organisation. So job descriptions for managers should concentrate on responsibilities, not duties.

JOB DESCRIPTIONS FOR SALARIED JOBS

Job descriptions for salaried jobs in schools should recognise the fact that management jobs exist not only to perform prescribed tasks, but also to play a part in leading whole-school development. Environment and circumstance change from school to school and from headteacher to headteacher, but the basic *raisons d'etre* remain the same. A job description should clarify that which an incumbent is paid to accomplish. It is the legal basis for agreement between the incumbent and the employer, so it should be a statement about goals and objectives, and give external stakeholders like parents and governors a clear and understandable picture of the nature and scope of the job.

Intellectual capital requires tacit understandings to be made explicit so that a school has a memory of what every employee does and how. Apart from their obvious legal significance, job descriptions are part of that process of record keeping. In general, they should:
- Specify why a job exists and its primary objectives.
- List accountabilities and the impact of the job on the mission of the school; in other words, the effect the job has on outcomes. An incumbent or a prospective incumbent should be made aware of what must be achieved in order to fulfil the primary objective of the job.
- Specify the extent of the job's freedom to act, and the nature and sources of control limiting the incumbent's ability to take decisions.
- Specify the role of the job in the overall scheme of things and the environment in which the incumbent is expected to operate.
- Bring out the technical, managerial, problem solving and human relations skills required. (These terms and their measurement are discussed below).
- Give a general idea of the magnitude of the job, and its prescribed and discretionary elements. The *discretionary* content of a job consists of those elements where choice is left to an incumbent and where the best course of action must be chosen from alternatives. It is the part that is perceived by incumbents to be their level of work. The *prescribed* content, on the other hand, consists of those elements about which an incumbent has no choice.

- Specify the size, scope and nature of each subordinate position reporting to the job. Relationships to and dependence upon other jobs should be clearly stated.
- Define the job in its own terms and not solely in terms of how it assists or relates to a more senior position.
- Make it known what is needed by way of education, experience, know-how and human relations skills to do the job to an acceptable standard.
- Describe the types of policy and procedure that the incumbent is expected to initiate, interpret or work within.
- State the type of guidance, supervision and direction that will be given to the incumbent.

Most schools rely on government circulars regarding conditions of employment for their generic job descriptions. If these are not used as the basis for employment, legal advice should be taken on their replacement. If there are specific personal characteristics associated with the probability of success in doing a job, they should be included in the job description and defined relative to some standard of success; for example, the completion of a professional qualification.

In schools, job descriptions form the basis of the professional agreement that exists between teachers and heads. Additionally, they give colleagues and outsiders a clear understanding of each role within the school and clarify accountability for outcomes. While the changing needs of schools mean that some adjustments usually have to be made to job descriptions over time, at any given time they should give accurate interim snapshots of jobs as they are currently constituted. They should state the effect of the job on the quality and quantity of the educational provision to students and how the job's primary objectives affect the school's mission.

Accountability - answerability for results and consequences - is related to the opportunity an employee has to generate important outcomes for a school. The extent to which he or she is free to act is therefore inversely related to the extent to which personal or procedural control exists. Responsibility influences the extent to which an employee is free to choose from alternatives. It may be shared or individually held, advisory or executive, and a job description should be clear about it. It should explain existing (or proposed) school management structures within which incumbents are expected to operate. Among other things, it should mention whether a senior management team exists at the school, who has membership of it and the division of responsibilities within it.

The discretionary element of a job is difficult to describe fully in a job description, because the relationship between the incumbent and the job is not yet fully established. However, an initial job description should give some indication as to the areas in which an incumbent can reasonably expect to exercise discretion, if not immediately then at some future stage. The description of the discretionary element is more than just an addendum to the job description. The discretionary element is the part of the job which gives the greatest satisfaction to employees and most enhances the quality of the work done, irrespective of quantity, so a description of it should be prepared with due care.

The preparation of a job description requires objectivity. It is the job that is of interest, not the job holder. This can be problematic because sometimes a position is exaggerated in importance and at other times it is deprecated. Either way, a job description must grasp the factual aspects of a job and extraneous details should be avoided. The description should be brief to force precise and clear thinking, and be written in a crisp style. Facts about the job should be recorded, but not conclusions about its efficacy, and if many job descriptions are to be written, a uniform layout and style is best.

THE MEASUREMENT OF RESPONSIBILITY

Central to the idea of job evaluation and responsibility analysis is the question of determining appropriate payment and status for individuals in their jobs. This is an emotive issue, questioning as it does an employee's security, value and usefulness to others, but before it can even be attempted, it is necessary to distinguish between level and quantity of work. *Level of work* is a measure of the size and intensity of responsibility in a job; *quantity of work* is the amount of work done irrespective of level of responsibility. Research shows that level of work rather than quantity is the aspect of a job that employees think merits differentiation in status or pay (Jaques, 1956). Most people have an intuitive idea about the relative importance of jobs, and critics of job evaluation and responsibility analysis say that to try to quantify it further is undesirable and even impossible. But some degree of differentiation has to be achieved. Typically, *job evaluation* ranks jobs by seniority for the purposes of establishing a hierarchy, whereas *job analysis* additionally quantifies the differential between them; in other words, places a numerical value on each job in an organisation. The complexity of the job and the organisation will determine which is the more appropriate tool in each case.

Job content changes over time, as do job titles, so it is important to have yardsticks that measure level of work which are flexible enough to adapt to changing circumstances. Two common (but frequently ineffective) ones are *work yardsticks* and *personal yardsticks*, which are discussed immediately below, but a more accurate and equitable approach to gauging level of work is to use the concepts of *maximum time span of discretion* and *range of level of work*, which are explored later.

Work and personal yardsticks

Work yardsticks make comparisons between jobs on the basis of the responsibilities they have in common. Included are factors like physical amount of work, accuracy and speed required in the job, number of subordinates, seriousness of consequences if negligent, complexity, and the value of the materials with which the incumbent works. It is a simplistic view. To take an example: if working to very fine tolerances is valued in an organisation, it should command higher pay. But fine tolerance is often merely a question of setting a machine for accuracy, rather than something that confers any credit on the operator, so the seemingly simple proposition that accuracy is good and should be rewarded is too simplistic to be fair.[24]

Personal yardsticks, on the other hand, make comparisons between jobs on the basis of the personal characteristics employees need in order to do the job effectively. Included are factors like training, educational qualifications, experience, reliability, determination and imagination. Personal yardsticks are really no more accurate than

---

[24] The example also serves to illustrate how technological advances can undermine a traditional view of work; in this case, that accuracy implies craftsmanship. Jobs change and therefore so should job descriptions. Old assumptions do not remain constant over time.

work yardsticks because it is impossible to compare - never mind measure - the relative merits of different personality traits. For example, a comparison between life experience and formal education cannot be meaningful; how can a sensible comparison be made between the number of years an employee spends teaching and the number of years another employee spends studying in university?

In most cases, both personal and work yardsticks fail even to give the illusion of objectivity. They are clearly not adequate measures of job worth.

The maximum time-span of discretion

The level of work in a job can be assessed by teasing out the discretionary content of the job, evaluating the mechanisms used to review the use of discretion by the incumbent and then discovering the maximum time that elapses during which the incumbent is authorised or expected to use discretion in relation to his or her responsibilities.

The *prescribed* content of a teaching job consists of those elements about which the teacher has no choice. There are normally two factors which remove the element of discretion: the fact that targets are set by the head or a line manager and not by the subordinate teacher; and the fact that the methods by which the desired outcomes are to be achieved are more or less predetermined.

The *discretionary* content of a job, on the other hand, consists of those elements about which the teacher has freedom of choice; in other words, those elements for which the work itself does not automatically determine the best method. The discretionary part of a job is the part that is least apparent to the incumbent. Discretion is seldom perceived as such because exercising judgement is something that is taken for granted.

Whatever the relative sizes of the discretionary and prescribed components of a job, a period of time elapses before the effects of discretion become apparent to a superior. This is what is meant by *time-span of discretion* and the maximum for any given job is a measure of the value of that job to an organisation. For example, in business, it may take several weeks before the return of unsatisfactory merchandise alerts a sales manager to a production problem. Or in a school setting, it may take a period of time for the inappropriate behaviour of a teacher to come to the attention of a head or deputy say.

Serious errors of judgement result in quicker reviews of discretion because consequences can then come to light sooner. Marginal errors do not attract the same attention unless consciously sought out, but cumulatively they do have a significant effect - a festering incompetence - if a long period of time elapses between error and effect. A headteacher can keep time-span of discretion to a minimum by reviewing reports as soon as they arrive or can lengthen it by postponing a review, tending towards the latter as confidence in the work of a subordinate increases. Traditionally, a job with a maximum time-span of discretion of less than one month is not regarded as carrying any managerial responsibility.

Review of work by a manager: The mechanisms by which a manager - defined as one who has authority over subordinates in the sense of selecting them and assessing their work - reviews an incumbent's use of discretion, can be divided into two categories: a direct review of work by a manager and an indirect review. A *direct* review of work occurs when all discretionary elements are examined by the relevant line manager.

Merely countersigning something does not constitute a review, nor is it sufficient for incumbents to submit, say, regular reports where the incumbents themselves decide what to include and what to leave out.[25]

An *indirect* review of work occurs when the outcome of work done by an incumbent moves unreviewed to the headteacher or a manager outside the direct line of command. For example, in business, a sales manager might review discretion in the production area by examining the amount of faulty merchandise returned. Or a headteacher might review the work of a teacher after dealing with a complaint from a parent.

Measuring the relative status of jobs: The prescribed element of a job should not be used as an index of importance or as a determinant of status or remuneration. Even in the simplest of jobs, like a clerk putting a decimal point in the wrong place, a tiny mistake can lead to disaster on an organisation-wide scale. It confuses matters to talk about the prescribed elements of jobs when comparing them; factors such as reliability, accuracy and qualifications only serve to group different jobs together under a convenient title, nothing more. The relative importance of jobs should only be judged by the amount of discretion exercised. This in turn requires accurate job descriptions so that discretionary components can be compared across jobs. Every teaching job has a discretionary component, though it is usually hidden from all but the teacher and the headteacher or line manager. If a job becomes so automatic that it no longer has any discretionary element, then it should no longer exist as a job for a teacher.

Generally, the higher the rank of a job, the greater the maximum time-span of discretion, and time-spans of discretion decrease as one goes down the ranks. This is inevitable, as a manager could not reasonably work at a shorter time-span of discretion than a subordinate, since the former must oversee the latter. In education, as in industry, employees with similar time-spans of discretion, irrespective of rank, typically claim parity of status and remuneration. Conversely, incumbents whose remuneration is perceived as being below that commensurate with their time-spans of discretion think themselves unfairly treated, and research shows they are the major instigators of grievance procedures (Jaques, 1956).[26]

Workers and jobs can be grouped by like time-spans of discretion and an increase in an employee's time-span of discretion within the group is what defines an increase in workload. And if such an increase in workload brings the teacher or worker to the next higher-ranking group, there should be formal promotion. In fact, promotion can be defined as the movement from one group to another with a longer time-span of discretion.

The elements of a job that confer status and cause difficulties: Organisations such as schools face difficulties as a result of changes in political climate, the need for continuous professional development and the general expansion and contraction of the system. Changes nationally in the status and remuneration of teachers and local changes in personnel are fluctuations that can subject a school to pressures that disturb it.

---

[25] Guidelines as to the format and content of reports should always be prescribed by the reviewing manager.

[26] In fact, Jaques could accurately predict a worker's remuneration given the worker's time-span of discretion and whether he or she was content or not. All of which brought Jaques to the conclusion that maximum time-span of discretion was an accurate measure of level of work.

Change cannot be managed unless and until it is recognised. Usually and unfortunately, it is noticed first by the effect it has on operations. In schools for example, teachers and support staff may feel dissatisfied as a result of performing well at a new higher level while being retained at an old status level; or conversely some employees may be unable to cope in new positions because an unrecognised promotion has occurred. Re-grades must take place when they are warranted, and when they do, they should be overt and agreed.

Occasionally, amount and level of work increase simultaneously without incumbents becoming aware of it (or compensated for it) until subordinates end up doing similar work to managers but without the status or pay. In such a scenario, found predominantly in schools that have expanded rapidly over a short period of time, subordinates become like colleagues to a superior and the situation is embarrassing for all concerned. From the headteacher's point of view, grievances tend to become very disruptive; from the teacher's point of view, fair performance appraisal becomes impossible. Systems for reward and promotion operate best when limits are set on the level of work that managers have immediately under their command. Duties should either be redistributed so that relative levels are maintained, or if the level of work of subordinates moves above or below established parameters, new positions should be set up and subordinates promoted.

Reorganisation is also required where a manager has gone up a level and there have been accompanying pulls on associated subordinate jobs within the organisation, creating imbalances where some subordinates have been advanced to a higher rank and others have not. Generally, in such a situation, associated jobs should move up together, though not necessarily simultaneously, so that patterns of relativity are maintained.

Teachers and support staff usually have an intuitive grasp of the value of their own work in a school, which is kept current by the influx of new teachers and the exodus of old ones. Furthermore, incumbents test their current status and pay relative to similar positions in other schools by reading about them in newspapers or applying for them as they occur. It is a natural moderation process, the result of mobility of labour. So when a teacher or administrator advances in a personal capacity, but the level of work available within the school remains the same or decreases, that incumbent either leaves for another job or accepts work at a level below his or her full capacity, which leads to frustration.

Equally serious is the phenomenon of losing employees to another school who are working at a higher level than their rank demands. These are the people who keep the operational standards of a workforce high. The rump of what remains after they leave usually sees a dramatic fall-off in performance unless top-quality replacements are bought in. And difficulties can arise when such vacancies are filled from outside, especially when they command a higher remuneration than was the case previously. It is not that the new higher salary and status is unjustified - the job may have developed a scarcity value - but there can be an awareness among staff that the higher salary is no more than what should have been paid to the previous incumbent anyway if level of work had been properly assessed. In fact, the absence of reappraisal may have been the cause of the incumbent leaving in the first place, so it is understandable if it generates some resentment among those who remain. So promote and reward when it is merited; it costs as much not to in the long run!

Range of level of work

Increased sensitivity to the concept of maximum time-span of discretion brings another evaluative concept into focus - *range of level of work*. Range of level of work is the widest range within which work can be allocated to a teacher or administrator, from the lowest level compatible with the work merely being done to the highest level available to be assigned. Range of level of work cannot be expanded or contracted at will. The upper level is set by the availability of work, and the lower level by the fact that when an incumbent's supervisor is doing more than a certain maximum amount of reviewing, there is no time left to fulfil his or her own obligations. At this lower point, it is just as easy for a headteacher or line manager to do a subordinate's job as to supervise it.

The measurement of range of level of work requires heads and managers to specify the upper and lower limits to all the jobs they supervise and thus lay the foundation for an open and transparent system of appraisal. Maximum and minimum remuneration can be predicated on these limits and the advancement of teachers and support staff can be monitored as to the time they exceed the maximum level available, making them aware of their promotion prospects if they near or regularly exceed that upper limit.

MANUAL AND HOURLY-RATED WORK

Teachers and administrators comprise the bulk of a school's staff. Together they are responsible for the core activities of teaching and tracking. However, a school has hourly-rated employees too; ancillary and caretaking staff, and substitute cover teachers. Research has shown that concepts like time-span of discretion are not applicable to hourly-rated jobs where the maximum time-span of discretion is shorter than a couple of days. In jobs with such short time-spans of discretion there is a poor three-way correspondence between discretion, perceived responsibility and pay, so the concept of discretion as a responsibility-measuring instrument needs to be redefined.

The means for such an elaboration can be found by taking into account factors such as work scrappage and damage avoidance. *Work scrappage* is work rejected as not being up to standard. Traditionally, employees attach considerable importance to it and it is generally accepted within a workforce that too much scrappage may fairly lead to lower pay and even dismissal. The allied notion of *damage avoidance* is the amount of wastage that an incumbent is relied upon to avoid through the use of his or her own discretion. Jobs that carry greater amounts of damage avoidance are the ones that employees themselves consider should receive higher rates of pay.

In schools and colleges, the definition of scrappage can be extended to include wastage due to unworkability or lack of credibility; and the notion of damage avoidance can be extended to include a measure of the extent to which unwelcome interference with the efficient running of the school is avoided.

Together, the concepts of scrappage and damage avoidance give a measure of the responsibility carried in short time-span hourly-rated jobs, although their application to management of schools may not be immediately apparent. They are most easily associated with manual production jobs, but are nevertheless sustained in schools by the experience of headteachers and curriculum managers. Senior positions in schools are expected to produce plans, timetables, innovations and so on, almost totally without scrappage. Middle managers and classroom teachers, on the other hand, do not have the same high expectation imposed upon them, or at least not to the same extent. So, for example, a deputy head is expected to produce a near-flawless academic timetable at the first time of asking, but the Head of Sport is allowed considerable latitude in the planning of the annual sports day. Higher-ranking jobs carry a lower tolerance of scrappage and a greater expectation of damage avoidance.

The clichéd recommendation that headteachers should have a 'whole school view of things' is recognition that greater damage avoidance is expected from more senior post-holders. Headteachers and deputies are expected to manage, innovate and administer without interfering with those parts of the school that are otherwise functioning well, and having a whole school view allows them and only them to make that assessment. Positions of diminished managerial responsibility are allowed more inadvertent interference, because there is an acceptance that jobs with less discretion carry a lower expectation of what can be termed *interference avoidance*.

THE TOTALITY OF WORK

Work is the sum of the prescribed and discretionary activities that employees do in discharging their responsibilities, but what employees experience as level of work is only the discretionary part. Discretion is required whenever there is more than one way of doing a job and is therefore concerned only with those aspects of a job where the teacher or administrator is allowed or expected to choose from alternative ways of doing things. In comparison, the prescribed portion of a job comprises those aspects of a job where the incumbent is prohibited from choosing[27] and where prescribed rules must be followed in pursuit of the objective.

The prescribed and discretionary components of a job interact as part of the totality of work in schools. The prescribed component can be thought of as constituting a boundary around the discretionary component, setting limits for it and stipulating what teachers and administrators must or must not do and the regulations to which they must conform. Within these prescribed limits, incumbents can and must use their discretion in selecting the best course of action from alternatives.

Setting confinements on a job is not necessarily a bad thing. It allows teachers and administrators to concentrate their judgement on their own fields of operation. Routines and procedures can be liberating, and it is nearly always the case that a complete absence of them leads to inefficiency.

Decision making and choice

Management in schools involves selecting the best course of action from those available and rejecting the alternatives, and only when a task is complete is it possible to put everything into perspective and discover which action would have made the task easier. In jobs with long time-spans of discretion, there is often more than one task to be done at any given time and decisions with respect to entirely different topics have to be made in quick succession. In such circumstances, better choices may remain unrecognised for a long period of time. There is a fine balance to be struck between on the one hand selecting a course of action immediately in order to get a job done and on the other, experimenting with new (informed) approaches in the hope that one of them will do the same job more effectively.

---

[27] In non-manual work, this 'choosing process' is what we call decision making.

When the best course of action is so obvious that it no longer requires an effort of choosing, a job has become too easy and is not worthy of a manager's time; when it presents alternative courses of action that are so similar that there is no perceived difference between them and all appear equally attractive, the job has become too complex and decision making is reduced to gambling.

Time-span capacity and job size

The capacity to tolerate uncertainty plays an important part in a teacher's capacity to do work. As tolerance of uncertainty grows, a greater capacity develops to put off decisions in the hope of something better. *Time-span capacity* is the length of time an incumbent is able to tolerate the delaying effects of exercising discretion; in other words, the length of time that an incumbent can postpone a necessary event.

The capacity to exercise discretion for longer or shorter periods of time is a function of an employee's ability to anticipate events that are consequent on action. The further ahead consequences are projected in the mind's eye, the less clear they become; and the greater a teacher's time-span capacity, the greater is his or her ability to use past experience as a bridge for uncertainty.

Maximum time-span capacity is a measure of the *size* of a job. The greater the tolerance for making decisions in the face of continuing uncertainty the more senior the position. When managers talk of being 'weighed down with responsibility' they reflect the fact that they experience too much uncertainty for too long and they feel insecure as a result.

Work is a kind of investment behaviour for schools, investing in staff foresight and the ability of teachers and administrators to lengthen their time-span capacities. As such it is a form of intellectual capital. The bigger the job, the more complex the decision tree, the longer the required period of foresight and the greater the uncertainty. A characteristic feature of management and leadership in schools is the proliferation of alternatives in the decision making process and the complexity of selecting one course of action from among many without the benefit of scientific calculation. Good educational decisions require a considerable amount of foresight; school jobs are big jobs even by commercial standards.

Time-span capacity and age

Research suggests that time-span capacity - the toleration of uncertainty - increases with age until middle age and then slows down, though it depends on the level at which an incumbent is operating. For school employees operating at low time-span levels, the growth in capacity tails off sooner, which suggests a need for two differentiating concepts: *current time-span capacity* and *potential time-span capacity*. In a way, the difference between the sum of current and potential time-span capacities is a measure of the intellectual capital of a school, and the job of school management is to devise interventions so that potential is both developed and realised.

An employee's time-span capacity exerts a strong influence on the level of work an employee seeks out, even without intervention by management. An ambitious teacher or administrator will naturally (though perhaps subconsciously) come to a job that satisfies his or her current time-span capacity until a level of work is eventually reached that corresponds to it. Current time-span capacity increases with learning and it will eventually outgrow its current position so that an employee looks to move up or move on. Time-span capacity is the engine of ambition, and headteachers should have a promotion system in place that recognises the benefits to the school of restless learning and the necessity for appropriate reward. A teacher or member of the support staff in a job matching his or her current time-span capacity, with a structured opportunity to change job as capacity increases, will be content. If the work is higher or lower than current time-span capacity, the incumbent will make adjustments to work at the appropriate level, by pressing on with special effort when working above current capacity or by off-loading responsibility to colleagues in the other case. Like tension in an elastic medium, the further an employee is removed from the correct level of work, the greater will be the employee's effort to get back to it, and there will be confrontation if barriers are erected to that realignment.

The pressure to work at the correct time-span level
Teachers and administrators exert pressure on management to work at their correct time-span capacities by seeking job change within and without the school, by attending training courses and by obtaining additional qualifications. Unfortunately, it is common for many teachers to then change careers, despite an initial drop in status and remuneration. An analogous situation exists in the industrial sector, though typically employees remain in position while feeling that their jobs have 'grown out from under them' as a result of expansion or automation. In both cases, fear causes inertia, which manifests itself later as resistance to change.
At other times, employees permanently accept work of shorter time-span capacity than is warranted. This is not peculiar to schools or industry; abnegation of advancement occurs everywhere. In a school setting, the motive usually offered by way of excuse is that the employee has put aside advancement in order to maintain friendships, to avoid parting from colleagues or to pursue existing interests in return for greater emotional return (Mant, 1969). Research from the industrial sector suggests that these excuses do not stand up to close scrutiny; the majority of employees who abnegate responsibility are in fact incapable of coping with increased responsibility.

The desire to have freedom to act independently is a powerful driving force behind ambition. In schools, few teachers or administrators take pleasure in the constant review of work by managers which is part and parcel of holding a junior position. However, too much responsibility leads to anxiety and this creates a tension for employees between the uncertainty that breeds a desire for supervision and the ambition that encourages independence and increases morale. It is unlikely that any organisation where there is an absence of ambition and low morale will survive, so it is for managers to see to it that fear and anxiety do not blight the ambition of junior staff. In schools (and universities) particularly, there is peer pressure to accept additional responsibility in a way that does not exist in a commercial setting. Teachers want to see school-wide difficulties overcome as effectively as possible and there is a general expectation in staff common rooms that those with the capability to solve problems should use their abilities *pro bono*. Research suggests that frustration is most common in schools where ordinary classroom teachers foresee difficulties that managers do not, and have the wherewithal to resolve them, but do not or cannot because of their relatively junior status.

Time-span capacity and growth

Whether a school grows or not depends, among other things, on the collective time-span capacity of its senior management. If management's time-span capacity is growing beyond the level of work available, management will grow the organisation; if management's time-span capacity is stable, the school will be stable; if management's time-span capacity is growing too slowly for the available level of work, the organisation will contract. And since time-span capacity is related to age, examining the age profile of managers with respect to the levels of work they discharge can be an important mechanism by which the stability and potential of a school is judged. A growing school should have a wide age profile within its senior management team, and promotion solely on the basis of seniority should not be the norm.

SUMMARY

A job is a set of recognisable, recurring, non-exceptional duties and responsibilities, and a job description is a public agreement between an employee and an employer. A job description should give external stakeholders a clear and understandable picture of the nature and scope of a job. It should state the primary objectives of the job and give a general idea of its prescribed and discretionary elements.

It is important to have a yardstick to measure level of work that is flexible enough to adapt to changing circumstances. The most accurate approach is to use the concepts of maximum time span of discretion and range of level of work.

The level of responsibility in a job can be assessed by discovering the maximum time that elapses during which an incumbent is expected to use discretion in relation to his or her responsibilities. The discretionary content of a job consists of those elements about which an incumbent has freedom of choice and for which the work itself does not automatically determine the best method. A job's time-span of discretion is the period of time that elapses before the effects of discretion become apparent to a manager, and the maximum for any given job is a measure of the value of that job to an organisation. A manager can keep it to a minimum by reviewing reports as soon as they arrive or can lengthen it by postponing a review of reports, tending towards the latter as confidence in the work of subordinates increases. The higher the rank of a job, the longer the maximum time-span of discretion. Occasionally, a job's level of responsibility increases without incumbents being aware of it or compensated for it, until eventually subordinates are doing similar work to a manager but without the status or pay. In such a scenario, grievances tend to become disruptive and performance appraisal impossible.

Range of level of work is the widest range within which work can be allocated to an incumbent, from the lowest level compatible with the work merely being done to the highest level available to be assigned. Range of level of work cannot be expanded or contracted at will. The upper level is set by the availability of work, and the lower level by the fact that when an incumbent's supervisor is doing more than a certain maximum amount of reviewing, there is no time to fulfil his or her own obligations. Maximum and minimum remuneration can be fixed on these limits.

For jobs with time-spans of discretion shorter than a few days, it is necessary to take into account factors such as work scrappage and damage avoidance. Work scrappage is work rejected as not being up to standard; damage avoidance is the amount of wastage that incumbents are relied upon to avoid through the use of their own discretion. Jobs that carry the greatest amounts of damage avoidance are the ones that should receive higher rates of pay. Together, the concepts of scrappage and damage avoidance give a measure of responsibility for hourly-rated jobs.

Decision making is about selecting the best course of action from alternatives and rejecting the rest. Only when a decision is made is it possible to discover which alternative might have made the task easier; better alternatives may remain unrecognised for a long period of time. The capacity to tolerate such uncertainty plays a part in an employee's capacity to be effective. As tolerance of uncertainty grows, a capacity develops to put off decisions with the prospect of something better. Time-span capacity is the length of time an incumbent is able to tolerate the delaying effects of discretion. The greater the tolerance for delaying decisions in the face of continuing uncertainty the more senior the position.

An employee's tolerance for uncertainty exerts a strong influence on the level of work he or she seeks out. An ambitious employee will come naturally to a job that satisfies his or her current time-span capacity, until a level of work is eventually reached that corresponds to it. Time-span capacity is the engine of ambition and schools should have promotion systems in place that recognise the benefits of restless learning and reward it. Management is not just about thought and talk. Real consequences follow poor judgements: work has to be re-done, time is wasted and in schools, pupils fail. Giving someone a job is handing part of an organisation to that employee. It is important for managers to understand what makes it a success.

CHAPTER 4

A new Profile Guide Chart Method for job evaluation in schools

> When you wish to instruct, be brief; that men's minds take in quickly what you say, learn its lesson, and retain it faithfully. Every word that is unnecessary only pours over the side of a brimming mind.
>
> *Cicero, 106 BC - 43 BC.*

INTRODUCTION

There are three general approaches to the analysis of jobs. The first, *task-centred job analysis*, describes work in terms of the outcomes to be achieved, which are themselves enumerated by carrying out a functional analysis of the job or by compiling a task checklist. Task-centred job analysis is detailed and specific, but is limited in its ability to identify similarities across sectors or between job types.

The second, *behaviour-centred job analysis*, describes work in terms of processes and behaviours. It focuses on the job holder rather than on job outcomes. It is less specific than the task-centred approach, but more transferable across different sectors and jobs, enabling comparisons to be made and similarities identified.

The third, *trait-centred job analysis*, describes work in terms of the personality traits required to successfully perform the job's functions. This approach suffers from the disadvantage of having to find a direct correspondence between job content and human attributes.

Job evaluation is a form of task-centred analysis. It is basically a systematic way of determining the relative importance of jobs by describing each one piecemeal in terms of its component parts. It is a derivative of the classical school of management and is rooted in the logic of bureaucracy. As a result - and this is its shortcoming - it regards job assessment as a particularly rational thing, but it is nevertheless a distinctive and helpful perspective on understanding the essence of a job from the point of view of an organisation.

The first step in job evaluation is the preparation of a job description. Each job is formally described according to its duties, requirements and responsibilities. Job evaluation measurement techniques then determine the value of each to the organisation, after which they are all cross-checked and correlated.

The manner of carrying out the second step – the job evaluation measurement – is what distinguishes one type of job evaluation from another. There are three main categories (see Figure 8):

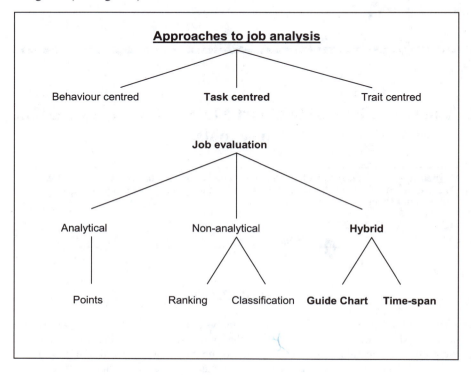

Figure 8. A typology of approaches to job analysis

- *Analytical methods*, which break down jobs into component factors. The most popular analytical approach is to use a *points rating* scheme, which involves choosing compensatable factors such as skill, effort and responsibility, and attaching weights to them according to their perceived importance to the organisation.
- *Non-analytical methods*, which compare jobs in a holistic way. The most popular non-analytical approaches are *ranking schemes* and *classification schemes*. In the former, jobs are ranked from the highest to the lowest, based on an assessment of each job as a whole and not as an amalgam of component factors. In the latter, jobs are divided into classes or families, each of which

has a generic classification. Each job is then matched to the nearest class according to its duties.

- *Hybrid methods* are combinations of analytical and non-analytical approaches. They include the *Time-span of Discretion* approach described in the last chapter and *Profile Guide Chart* schemes.

A new (hybrid) Profile Guide Chart scheme for evaluating jobs in schools, which takes account of concepts like time-span of discretion, is developed below.

A PROFILE GUIDE CHART METHOD FOR USE IN SCHOOLS

The Profile Guide Chart method of job evaluation was conceived in the 1950s and has its roots in earlier Factor Comparison methods. It is widely regarded as the industry standard. The fundamental ways in which jobs can equate with (or differ from) one another are arranged on scales and a *Guide Chart* is put together consisting of two or more of these scales brought together in a grid. While each scale is defined only in general terms, each step on it is a progressive refinement in detail.

An evaluation system based on Guide Charts has a number of underpinning features, some of which require an understanding of scaling techniques as well as an understanding of organisations:

- There are many factors to be considered in the evaluation of a job, but the most important three are: the knowledge required to do the job; the kind of thinking required to solve the problems commonly faced in the job; and the responsibilities assigned to the job.
- A good evaluation system should not only be able to rank jobs in order of importance, but be able to measure their relative size; in other words, a good evaluation system should be able to measure the *significant difference* between jobs.
- The focus of job evaluation as a process is on the nature and requirement of a job, not on the skills and characteristics of its incumbent.

These underpinning features suggest a three-factor codification of jobs,[28] each of which can be compared to another with respect to what is considered common to all jobs; *Know-how*, *Problem solving* and *Accountability*. Each of these three factors has a corresponding Guide Chart to measure it.

Know-how

Know-how is the sum of every kind of knowledge and skill required for the acceptable performance of a job, however obtained (see Figure 9). Its three dimensions are Practical Scientific know-how, Managerial know-how and Human Relations skills:

- ***Practical Scientific know-how*** is the sum of scientific knowledge and experience within the field of education and teaching. It consists largely of specialised techniques and procedures, and can be categorised according to its

---

[28] A fourth factor, *Working Conditions*, can be introduced, if required, to comply with employment legislation for hazardous jobs, unpleasant conditions or for jobs which are physically demanding.

variety (or width) and complexity (or depth). Exemplars are given on Figure 10.

Some jobs require a little knowledge of many things; others require a great deal of knowledge about relatively few things. To reflect this fact, Practical Scientific know-how, on the vertical axis of Figure 9, ranges from *Basic Understanding* (A) to *Professional Eminence* (H).

- *Managerial know-how* is the ability to integrate and harmonise the diverse functions of a job in order to produce desired outcomes for the school as an organisation. It involves, in some combination, skills in planning, organising, co-ordinating, executing, evaluating, directing and controlling resources. Managerial know-how is on the upper horizontal axis of Figure 9 and ranges from *Non-supervisory* (N) to *Total* (V)

- *Human Relations skills* are comprised of the person-to-person and social skills that are essential to jobs involving work with other people. It is on the lower horizontal axis of Figure 9 and ranges from *Basic* (1) to *Critical* (3).

Problem solving

Problem solving is the original use of know-how to identify, define and resolve problems (see Figure 11). Teachers think with what they know, even in the most creative aspects of what they do, so problem solving can be thought of as a simple percentage of know-how.

Problem solving is less important whenever results can be obtained by the automatic application of skill, rather than by the application of a thinking process to knowledge, so this Guide Chart measures the extent to which thinking processes must be applied to a job's required knowledge in order to get the desired results. It has two dimensions: Thinking Environment and Thinking Challenge:

- *Thinking Environment* represents the extent to which assistance is available from colleagues or from precedent. This dimension is on the vertical axis of Figure 11 and ranges from *Highly Structured* (A) to *Abstract* (H).

- *Thinking Challenge* represents the complexity and novelty of the thinking that is required in a job. It is represented on the horizontal axis of Figure 11 and ranges from *Repetitive* (1) to *Uncharted* (5).

GUIDE CHART FOR EVALUATING KNOW-HOW

MANAGERIAL KNOW-

PRACTICAL SCIENTIFIC KNOW-HOW	N. Non-supervisory — Performance of activities as an individual, not as a professional manager.			I. Minimal — Performance or direction of a group of duties similar in content & aims, being aware of other school activities.			II. Related — Incumbent directs a team with variety of duties & aims. Or guides group of like sub-duties across several teams.		
	1	2	3	1	2	3	1	2	3
A. Basic understanding: Incumbent has a basic familiarity with simple school routines.	38	43	50	50	57	66	66	76	87
	43	50	57	57	66	76	76	87	100
	50	57	66	66	76	87	87	100	115
B. Elementary skill / knowledge: Capable of carrying out standard school procedures. Use of simple programmes.	50	57	66	66	76	87	87	100	115
	57	66	76	76	87	100	100	115	132
	66	76	87	87	100	115	115	132	152
C. Intermediate skill / knowledge: Experienced in applying procedures with some deviation. Use of specialist programmes.	66	76	87	87	100	115	115	132	152
	76	87	100	100	115	132	132	152	175
	87	100	115	115	132	152	152	175	200
D. Extended skill / knowledge: Good at implementing school systems, with skills requiring technical knowledge.	87	100	115	115	132	152	152	175	200
	100	115	132	132	152	175	175	200	230
	115	132	152	152	175	200	200	230	264
E. Diverse / specialised: Understanding & skill in a variety of activities. Needs command of basic management theory.	115	132	152	152	175	200	200	230	264
	132	152	175	175	200	230	230	264	304
	152	175	200	200	230	264	264	304	350
F. Seasoned diverse / specialised: Needs command of management theory or a very experienced manager or both.	152	175	200	200	230	264	264	304	350
	175	200	230	230	264	304	304	350	400
	200	230	264	264	304	350	350	400	460
G. Broad or specialised mastery: Command of educational or management theory through professional development.	200	230	264	264	304	350	350	400	460
	230	264	304	304	350	400	400	460	528
	264	304	350	350	400	460	460	528	608
H. Professional eminence: Externally recognised expertise in some aspect of management or educational leadership.	264	304	350	350	400	460	460	528	608
	304	350	400	400	460	528	528	608	700
	350	400	460	460	528	608	608	700	800

1. Basic: Ordinary courtesy & effectiveness in dealing with colleagues.	**2. Important**: Influence teachers; management are important aspects of

HUMAN RELATIONS

Figure 9. Evaluating know-how in schools

HOW

III. Diverse — Incumbent directs a large team with various duties. Or guides some duties that affect all or most of the school.			IV. Broad — Incumbent directs a management team with large functional diversity. Or guides policy decisions that affect all or most of the school.			V. Total — Leadership of all management teams, functions, policies and decisions i.e. incumbent is acting as headteacher or chief executive.		
1	**2**	**3**	**1**	**2**	**3**	**1**	**2**	**3**
87	100	115	115	132	152	152	175	200
100	115	132	132	152	175	175	200	230
115	132	152	152	175	200	200	230	264
115	132	152	152	175	200	200	230	264
132	152	175	175	200	230	230	264	304
152	175	200	200	230	264	264	304	350
152	175	200	200	230	264	264	304	350
175	200	230	230	264	304	304	350	400
200	230	264	264	304	350	350	400	460
200	230	264	264	304	350	350	400	460
230	264	304	304	350	400	400	460	528
264	304	350	350	400	460	460	528	608
264	304	350	350	400	460	460	528	608
304	350	400	400	460	528	528	608	700
350	400	460	460	528	608	608	700	800
350	400	460	460	528	608	608	700	800
400	460	528	528	608	700	700	800	920
460	528	608	608	700	800	800	920	1056
460	528	608	608	700	800	800	920	1056
528	608	700	700	800	920	920	1056	1216
608	700	800	800	920	1056	1056	1216	1400
608	700	800	800	920	1056	1056	1216	1400
700	800	920	920	1056	1216	1216	1400	1610
800	920	1056	1056	1216	1400	1400	1610	1852

over & understanding of of subordinates & peers the job.	**3. Critical**: Advanced skills have been developed by incumbent in understanding & motivating people; extremely important for the job.

SKILLS

Figure 9 (<u>continued</u>). Evaluating know-how in schools

P R A C T I C A L S C I E N T I F I C K N O W - H O W	EVALUATING KNOW-HOW	EXEMPLARS
	A. Basic understanding: Incumbent has a basic familiarity with simple school routines.	**A. BASIC**: Roll books.
	B. Elementary skill / knowledge: Capable of carrying out standard school procedures. Use of simple programmes.	**B. ELEMENTARY**: Administrative returns.
	C. Intermediate skill / knowledge: Experienced in applying procedures with some deviation. Use of specialist programmes.	**C. INTERMEDIATE**: Timetable construction; organising events, but typically not designing them.
	D. Extended skill / knowledge: Good at implementing school systems, with skills requiring technical knowledge.	**D. EXTENDED**: Introducing established systems of pastoral care or administration.
	E. Diverse / specialised: Understanding & skill in a variety of activities. Needs command of basic management theory.	**E. DIVERSE**: Managing groups or fairly wide-ranging management activities.
	F. Seasoned diverse / specialised: Needs command of management theory or a very experienced manager or both.	**F. SEASONED**: Managing small changes and problems that are not everyday or predictable.
	G. Broad or specialised mastery: Command of educational or management theory through professional development.	**G. MASTERY**: Managing significant changes and problems that arise from the school being in unusual circumstances.
	H. Professional eminence: Externally recognised expertise in some aspect of management or educational leadership.	**H. EMINENCE**: Leading change in a school that is involved in some innovation or pilot programme; leading other schools in the area or nationally.

Figure 10. Evaluating know-how in schools

THINKING CHALLENGE

THINKING ENVIRONMENT

GUIDE CHART FOR EVALUATING PROBLEM-SOLVING	**1. Repetitive** Identical situations requiring the incumbent to make simple choices between known things.	**2. Patterned** Similar situations requiring the incumbent to make discriminating choices between known things.	**3. Varied** Differing situations requiring the incumbent to search for solutions within an area of known things.	**4. Adaptive** Variable situations requiring analytical, interpretive, evaluative and / or constructive thinking.	**5. Uncharted** New or non-recurring path-finding situations requiring development of new concepts & imaginative approaches.
A. Highly structured: Thinking within detailed school rules / instructions. Or constant supervision / help by head.	10% 12%	14% 16%	19% 22%	25% 29%	33% 38%
B. Routine: Thinking within detailed school practice. Or immediate help or illustrative examples available.	12% 14%	16% 19%	22% 25%	29% 33%	38% 43%
C. Semi-routine: Thinking within well-defined school procedures. Precedence helps or ready assistance.	14% 16%	19% 22%	25% 29%	33% 38%	43% 50%
D. Standardised: Thinking within substantially diverse procedures. Precedence helps or access to assistance.	16% 19%	22% 25%	29% 33%	38% 43%	50% 57%
E. Clearly defined: Thinking within a remit of the head towards specific goals. Guided a lot by practice & precedent.	19% 22%	25% 29%	33% 38%	43% 50%	57% 66%
F. Generally defined: Thinking within head's remit towards specific goals. Some intangible unstructured aspects.	22% 25%	29% 33%	38% 43%	50% 57%	66% 76%
G. Broadly defined: Thinking in education management concepts. Broadly towards school goals. Much intangible.	25% 29%	33% 38%	43% 50%	57% 66%	76% 87%
H. Abstract: Thinking within education or school management philosophy or human relations theory.	29% 33%	38% 43%	50% 57%	66% 76%	87%

Figure 11. Evaluating problem-solving in schools

Accountability

Accountability is the extent to which incumbents are answerable for their actions and the consequences of their actions. It is the measured effect of a job on the output of the school (see Figure 12) and is related to the opportunity the job provides for bringing about results that are of importance to the school. There are three components to accountability, in the following decreasing order of importance: Freedom to Act, Job Impact and Magnitude.

- **Freedom to Act** is the degree to which personal or procedural control exists or does not exist in a job. It is represented on the vertical axis of Figure 12 and ranges from *Restricted* (R) to *General Guidance* (H). Exemplars are given on Figure 13.

- **Job Impact** is the degree to which a job affects organisational outcomes. It is reckoned as being in one of four categories:

  Primary Impact (P) occurs when a job exercises control over the resources and activities that produce the end-results. Employees answer to Primary Impact jobs.

  Shared Impact (S) occurs when a job that controls the resources that produce the end-results is shared equally with one other person, or where there is control of most but not all of the significant variables that bring about the end-results.

  Contributory Impact (C) occurs when a job provides advice, interpretation or support to others so that the desired results can be achieved.

  Ancillary Impact (A) occurs when supplementary assistance, information or an auxiliary service is given in support of others.

  Job impact is represented on the lower horizontal axis of Figure 12. There are A, C, S and P categories in each of the six Magnitude categories (see below).

- **Magnitude** represents the extent to which the school is encompassed by a job. For example, deputy headship usually encompasses whole-school duties, but can in other cases be confined to the Sixth Form or the Lower School. This dimension is represented on the upper horizontal axis of Figure 12, parallel to the Impact dimension. It ranges in six steps from *Very Small* (1) to *Very Large* (6) and corresponds to the UK government's (DfES) categorisation of schools by size.

SCHOOL SIZE

GUIDE CHART FOR EVALUATING ACCOUNTABILITY	1. Very small — School Group 1				2. Small — School Group 1				3. Medium small — School Group 3	
Impact =	A	C	S	P	A	C	S	P	A	C
R. Restricted: Duties subject to explicit instructions or constant personal or procedural supervision.	5	7	9	12	7	9	12	16	9	12
	6	8	10	14	8	10	14	19	10	14
	7	9	12	16	9	12	16	22	12	16
A. Prescribed: Duties subject to direct detailed instructions or very close supervision.	8	10	14	19	10	14	19	25	14	19
	9	12	16	22	12	16	22	29	16	22
	10	14	19	25	14	19	25	33	19	25
B. Controlled: Duties subject to instructions, established routines or close supervision.	12	16	22	29	16	22	29	38	22	29
	14	19	25	33	19	25	33	43	25	33
	16	22	29	38	22	29	38	50	29	38
C. Standardised: Duties subject to standard practices & procedures, & supervision of progress & results.	19	25	33	43	25	33	43	57	33	43
	22	29	38	50	29	38	50	66	38	50
	25	33	43	57	33	43	57	76	43	57
D. Generally regulated: Duties subject to definite procedures. Supervision of short-term results.	29	38	50	66	38	50	66	87	50	66
	33	43	57	76	43	57	76	100	57	76
	38	50	66	87	50	66	87	115	66	87
E. Directed: Duties subject to broad defined policy. Head directs incumbent's medium-term results.	43	57	76	100	57	76	100	132	76	100
	50	66	87	115	66	87	115	152	87	115
	57	76	100	132	76	100	132	175	100	132
F. General direction: Duties subject to functional policies. Head directs long-term results.	66	87	115	152	87	115	152	200	115	152
	76	100	132	175	100	132	175	230	132	175
	87	115	152	200	115	152	200	264	152	200
G. Guidance: Duties subject to the guidance of school policy & direction from head (or higher).	100	132	175	230	132	175	230	304	175	230
	115	152	200	264	152	200	264	350	200	264
	132	175	230	304	175	230	304	400	230	304
H. General guidance: Duties subject to guidance of educational policy & legal limits.	152	200	264	350	200	264	350	460	264	350
	175	230	304	400	230	304	400	528	304	400
	200	264	350	460	264	350	460	608	350	460
Impact =	A	C	S	P	A	C	S	P	A	C

The left margin reads vertically: **FREEDOM** (rows R–D) **TO ACT** (rows E–H).

A = ancillary   S = shared

C = contributory   P = primary

Figure 12. Evaluating accountability in schools

SCHOOL SIZE

3. Medium small		4. Medium large				1. Large				2. Very large			
School Group 3		School Group 4				School Group 5				School Group 6			
S	P	A	C	S	P	A	C	S	P	A	C	S	P
16	22	12	16	22	29	16	22	29	38	22	29	38	50
19	25	14	19	25	33	19	25	33	43	25	33	43	57
22	29	16	22	29	38	22	29	38	50	29	38	50	66
25	33	19	25	33	43	25	33	43	57	33	43	57	76
29	38	22	29	38	50	29	38	50	66	38	50	66	87
33	43	25	33	43	57	33	43	57	76	43	57	76	100
38	50	29	38	50	66	38	50	66	87	50	66	87	115
43	57	33	43	57	76	43	57	76	100	57	76	100	132
50	66	38	50	66	87	50	66	87	115	66	87	115	152
57	76	43	57	76	100	57	76	100	132	76	100	132	175
66	87	50	66	87	115	66	87	115	152	87	115	152	200
76	100	57	76	100	132	76	100	132	175	100	132	175	230
87	115	66	87	115	152	87	115	152	200	115	152	200	264
100	132	76	100	132	175	100	132	175	230	132	175	230	304
115	152	87	115	152	200	115	152	200	264	152	200	264	350
132	175	100	132	175	230	132	175	230	304	175	230	304	400
152	200	115	152	200	264	152	200	264	350	200	264	350	460
175	230	132	175	230	304	175	230	304	400	230	304	400	528
200	264	152	200	264	350	200	264	350	460	264	350	460	608
230	304	175	230	304	400	230	304	400	528	304	400	528	700
264	350	200	264	350	460	264	350	460	608	350	460	608	800
304	400	230	304	400	528	304	400	528	700	400	528	700	920
350	460	264	350	460	608	350	460	608	800	460	608	800	1056
400	528	304	400	528	700	400	528	700	920	528	700	920	1216
460	608	350	460	608	800	460	608	800	1056	608	800	1056	1400
528	700	400	528	700	920	528	700	920	1216	700	920	1216	1610
608	800	460	608	800	1056	608	800	1056	1400	800	1056	1400	1852
S	P	A	C	S	P	A	C	S	P	A	C	S	P

A = ancillary
C = contributory
S = shared
P = primary

Figure 12 (continued). Evaluating accountability in schools

	EVALUATING ACCOUNTABILITY	EXEMPLARS
F R E E D O M **T O** **A C T**	**R. Restricted**: Duties subject to explicit instructions or constant personal or procedural supervision.	Admin tasks done immediately upon request from the head or by events. There is explicit instruction as to method and outcome, both of which are checked constantly. E.g. organising cover for a class group unexpectedly left without a teacher.
	A. Prescribed: Duties subject to direct detailed instructions or very close supervision.	Admin tasks that come with detailed instructions, but no explanation or relevancy explained. Tasks purely bureaucratic. Head checks during the task or at certain stages. E.g. the preparation of a parents' evening.
	B. Elementary skill / knowledge: Duties subject to instructions & established routines or close supervision.	Admin tasks are checked before implementation. Head checks the internal checks in a summative way. Head gives general instruction as to the best method i.e. the established way of performing the tasks. E.g. checking department budgets for overspend.
	C. Standardised: Duties subject to standard practices & procedures & supervision of progress and results.	The admin tasks typically reveal errors within the current year, next term say, typically when a complaint is made. There is a standard practice that is normally followed. E.g. a problem in last term's rota was not corrected in the next version.
	D. Generally regulated: Duties subject to definite procedures & past precedent. Short-term supervision of results.	E.g. Weekly or termly rosters. Some staff politics is involved and / or the admin tasks reveal errors before next year's equivalent is done. Discretionary time-span of less than one academic year.
	E. Directed: Duties subject to broad practices & defined policy. Medium-term supervision of results by head.	E.g. Main timetable for the year. Head works out staffing & curricular implications while this job does the rooms, teachers, etc. There is no policy review at year-end, but there may be early warnings. Discretionary time-span of approximately one academic year.
	F. General directed: Duties subject to definite functional policies. Long-term supervision of results by head.	Not a decision-making job, but a functionary one. E.g. does the timetable, but does not make the curriculum decisions. Makes recommendations to the Head on staffing & other implications so there are long-term goals involved. Or admin tasks where errors are unnoticed for a year or longer, so there is a discretionary time-span of more than one academic year.
	G. Guidance: Duties subject to guidance of the school's policy & direction from the head.	E.g. makes the curriculum decisions in addition to doing the timetable say, but within existing school policy. Arranges subject options but from an existing list, say. Or constructs a pastoral programme, but within stated parameters that limit the freedom to act.
	H. General guidance: Duties subject to guidance of education policy, legal limits & school's mandate.	E.g. makes & implements policy decisions in curriculum, pastoral and / or other areas. E.g. does the timetable and also decides on the curriculum offered to various year groups.

Figure 13. Evaluating accountability in schools

THE SCALES ON THE GUIDE CHARTS

The scales on the Know-how and Accountability charts (Figure 9 and Figure 12) - but not on the Problem Solving chart (Figure 11) - are expandable to reflect the size and complexity of a school as an organisation; and the nomenclature can be adjusted to suit individual circumstance, which is called *sizing* the Guide Charts.

For each factor, the reading is a single number. The numbers on the charts increase at the rate of fifteen percent, except for the very small numbers, in order to conform to two general principles of psychometric scaling:

- *Weber's Law*, which states that when comparing objects, one perceives not actual difference but the ratio of difference to magnitude. So the relationship between numbers in more important than the numbers themselves.
- The concept of *Just Noticeable Difference*, which states that characteristic differences that are noticeable tend to be specific constant percentages. So an evaluator must have, say, a fifteen percent difference between job characteristics in order to notice that one job is bigger than another.

Instinctively, managers know the *shape* of jobs; up-hill, flat or down-hill. Using Guide Charts, jobs can be scientifically described on the basis of the relationship between Know-how, Problem Solving and Accountability. An *up-hill* job is one for which the Accountability score is greater than the Problem Solving score, a *down-hill* job is one in which the Accountability score is lower than the Problem Solving score, and a *flat* job is one in which the two are equal in size. So an up-hill job is one where results are more important than intensive thinking - an up-hill job is a *do* job - and a down-hill job is one where the use of knowledge through thinking is more important that answerability for results - a *think* job.

Job evaluation using Guide Charts is a measuring process, not a measuring instrument, which is why it is possible to modify the scales on the charts to reflect the character and structure of particular schools, and why the charts have the ability to absorb new information on job content over time. It is a relative, not an absolute, measuring process based on four beliefs:

- Every job requires some know-how, problem solving and accountability.
- Guide Chart scales reflect degrees to which these three factors are developed and used in a job.
- A relative rank order can be produced for jobs, and differences that reflect their relative importance can be measured.
- Guide Charts are driven by principles, rather than by immutable scales or rules, so the process of measurement can be adapted for use in different organisations.

POST EVALUATION CROSS CHECKS AND CORRELATION

The idea of shape is what gave the word 'profile' to the title of the Guide Charts, and it is shape that controls their relative calibration; in other words, the numbering patterns on the Guide Charts are set such that proper use produces scores for the factors which, when arrayed for a given job, produce a shape or profile that is recognisable to the incumbent. This provides important *post facto* checks to any evaluation: the profile or shape of a job should make sense, and the Guide Chart scores should be compared to scores for bigger, smaller and similar jobs to moderate the result. After a job has been evaluated, if the relationship between Problem Solving and Accountability does not fit the incumbent's perception, there is a strong possibility that an error has occurred. For example, school administration jobs should be 'do' jobs, curriculum innovation jobs should be 'think' jobs, and personnel and accounting jobs should be 'flat'. And each job should then be compared to others above and below it, in descending order say, to see if the scores in any of the three dimensions are overly high or low in comparison. These are what might be called *sore-thumb checks*.

Guide Chart job evaluation has a second check, that of *correlation*, which involves taking a sample of evaluations and comparing them with known jobs *in other organisations*. A correlation factor can then be worked out that allows a correspondence to be made between the two sets of jobs.
Correlation with jobs in other organisations is mostly used for the purpose of remuneration, comparing salaries in one organisation with those in another. However, it is important that two spurious effects are first eliminated from the comparison: the *halo effect*, where an incumbent's above-average performance in a job increases the score allocated to a job; and the *horns effect*, where an incumbent's below average performance decreases a score. Comparison should be between jobs, not between job-holders.

EXAMPLES OF EVALUATION USING GUIDE CHARTS

Example 1

Highfield School is a large comprehensive school with a Sixth Form of approximately 150 pupils, categorised as *Group 6* by the UK Department for Education and Skills (DfES). According to its most recent inspection report (from Ofsted, the UK Office for Standards in Education), it has a well-established senior management team with two deputy heads. The position of pastoral deputy, the more junior of the two, is being evaluated using the Guide Charts.
The job description is specific as to the deputy's sole and jointly held responsibilities. The incumbent is expected to undertake a significant amount of teaching. This will vary from year to year, so the exact whole-time equivalence is not made explicit in the job specification. The most important managerial functions of the job include the exploration, design, development and implementation of a new whole-school system to monitor pupil progress, and promoting that system among teaching and pastoral staff (see Figure 14, Panel 2).

PANEL 1

School: Highfield School   **Ofsted:** May 2001
Type: Comprehensive
Size: 1300   **Group:** 6

Salary for job: See separate file
Equivalent positions: 2 deputy heads
Membership of SMT: 7: H + 2DH + 3 Senior Teachers + operations manager

---

PANEL 2

Position: Deputy Head (Pastoral)
Duties mentioned in job description:
To raise achievement with regard to monitoring pupil progress.
To design & implement a new whole school system for monitoring pupil progress.
To develop base-line testing in Year 7.
To raise teacher awareness of the monitoring system and to gauge its effectiveness
To support teachers in their target setting.
To liaise with the curriculum deputy head.
To organise and chair meetings to discuss and disseminate policy.
To develop study programmes to encourage pupils.
To develop links with outside agencies.
To develop a range of celebratory events for achievement.
To work with department heads to ensure consistency.
To carry out administration for the post.
To assist the head in preparing reports.
To reinforce rules and ethos and to deal with discipline in Year 10.

PANEL 3

Personal qualities required: None specified in job description

---

PANEL 4

Guide Chart Analysis
Summary: To design, explore, develop, implement, monitor & support a whole-school system for monitoring pupil progress.

Know-how: F+; III; 3   608
Problem solving: F+; 4   (57%)   347
Accountability: F; 6; C+   460   **Total:**   1415

PANEL 5

Responsibility Analysis
Discretionary element: Large
Max time-span of discretion: Greater than 1 year
Range of level of work: Wide

Figure 14. Example 1 of a Guide Chart evaluation (Highfield School, deputy headship)

Responsibility Analysis: The job description is a thorough one and the responsibilities described in it are onerous and of fundamental importance to the mission of the school. The discretionary element of the job is *Large* and the maximum time-span of discretion for substantive tasks such as the design and implementation of a whole-school system is relatively long – *in excess of one year* – so a large Guide Chart score can be anticipated. The range of level of work is *Wide*, from assisting the head in the preparation of reports to the design of the whole-school system for monitoring pupil progress (see Figure 14, Panel 5).

Know-How: Since the job involves managing medium size change with unpredictable problems, and demands *at least* a good command of educational theory (see Figure 9 and Figure 10), the assessment of the Scientific Know-how required for the job is on the boundary of *Seasoned Diverse / Specialised* (F) and *Broad or Specialised Mastery* (G). The F+ and G- scores are the same (see Figure 9) so it can be scored as F+.
The job involves the direction of a large diverse school-wide team and affects the entire school, so Managerial Know-how is assessed as *Diverse* (III) (see Figure 9, upper horizontal axis).
Skills in motivating staff are *Critical* to the success of the introduction of the system so this is assessed as 3 (see Figure 9, lower horizontal axis).
Know-how is scored as 608 (see Figure 14, Panel 4).

Problem Solving: The job is under the head's direction towards the goal of developing a whole-school system and there are many intangible aspects to the undertaking, so the Thinking Environment is assessed as being in the upper reaches of *Generally Defined* (F) (see Figure 11). As the job demands interpretative and constructive thinking by the incumbent, the Thinking Challenge is assessed as *Adaptive* (4). It is not quite *Uncharted* (5) since whole-school systems can be imported from other schools. The thinking required is not path-finding, however imaginative it may turn out to be.
Problem Solving is scored as 57%. It is a percentage of Know-how and 57% of 608 is 347 (see Figure 14, Panel 4).

Accountability: The job is subject to functional policy as the head directs the incumbent towards the job's long-term goal. As the curriculum deputy is directed by the head rather than by general school policy, the Freedom to Act is classed as *General Direction* (F) rather than as *Guidance* (G) (see Figure 12 and Figure 13).
The Impact of the job is essentially advisory and supportive, particularly in the context of the management structure of the school, and it is not a position shared equally with another. So it is assessed as *Contributory* (C), but at the upper end (see Figure 12).
The size of the school places it in the *Very Large* (6) category (see Figure 12), so the Accountability score is 460 (see Figure 14, Panel 4).

PANEL 1

School: Shaftesbury Road School   **Ofsted:** January 2002
Type: 11-16 Comprehensive
Size: 1500   **Group:** 6

Salary for job: See separate file
Equivalent positions: Not documented
Membership of SMT: Not documented

PANEL 2

Position: Head of Key Stage 3
Duties mentioned in job description:
To be KS3 curriculum manager in all respects.
To coordinate the school development plan.
To develop & enhance lines of communication with partners & parents.
To lead teams, especially the pastoral team.
To take charge of school trips and visits.
To monitor discipline, behaviour & sanctions.

PANEL 3

Personal qualities required:
Proven management skills; good motivator of staff & pupils; a believer in equal opportunities; experience in more than one school; experience of mixed ability grouping.

PANEL 4

Guide Chart Analysis
Summary: Key Stage 3 curriculum and pastoral manager, and responsible for development planning.

Know-how: D; III; 2   264
Problem solving: D+; 3   (33%)   87
Accountability: E+; 6; C   304   **Total:** 655

PANEL 5

Responsibility Analysis
Discretionary element: Moderate
Max time-span of discretion: 1 year
Range of level of work: Medium

Figure 15. Example 2 of a Guide Chart evaluation (Shaftesbury Road School, Head of KS3)

Example 2

Shaftesbury Road School is a large 11-16 comprehensive school, categorised as *Group 6* by the (DfES). The current principal is in place one year. The most recent Ofsted report describes the school's catchment area as 'very disadvantaged' in socio-economic terms and the school has serious and frequent disciplinary problems. The inspection report identifies Key Stage 3 (KS3) - the first two years of secondary school - as being particularly weak and recommends that it be 'reviewed and restructured'. The position of Head of Key Stage 3 is being evaluated using the Guide Charts.

The job description describes the position as having a mixture of pastoral and curricular duties. The job is primarily intended to take responsibility for all matters relating to Key Stage 3 (See Figure 15, Panel 2).

> ***Responsibility Analysis:*** The discretionary element of the job is *Moderate* and the maximum time-span of discretion for the job's substantive tasks is approximately *one year*. Pupil cohorts make the transition from primary to secondary school and from KS3 to KS4 every year, so a modest Guide Chart score can be anticipated. The range of level of work is *Medium*, from managing KS3 to overseeing school visits (See Figure 15, Panel 5).
>
> ***Know-how:*** Since the job, at its highest level of work, requires technical knowledge skills and the ability to implement a school system for a particular year group (see Figure 9 and Figure 10), the assessment of Scientific Know-how required for the job is *Extended Skill / Knowledge* (D).
> The job involves the direction of a large diverse school-wide team, which affects the entire school, so Managerial Know-how is assessed as *Diverse* (III) on the upper horizontal axis of Figure 9.
> Skill in motivating staff is not critical to the job's success, but it is important that the incumbent has influence, so Human Relations Skills are assessed as *Important* (2) (see Figure 9, lower horizontal axis).
> Know-how is scored as 264 (see Figure 15, Panel 4).
>
> ***Problem Solving:*** The Thinking Environment is assessed as being at the upper end of *Standardised* (D) as the job involves thinking within diverse procedures with assistance readily available from the headteacher and the deputy (see Figure 11). It is likely to involve rapidly occurring unforeseen problems, mostly of a disciplinary or motivational nature, with solutions largely dictated by precedent and practice, and resolved quickly.
> The job requires the incumbent to search for solutions within a fairly confined experiential area, so Thinking Challenge is assessed as *Varied* (3).
> Problem Solving is scored as 33%. It is a percentage of Know-how and 33% of 264 is 87 (see Figure 15, Panel 4).
>
> ***Accountability:*** The job is subject to school policy and practices, and the head directs the incumbent towards medium-term goals; the long end of 'Medium', as some matters are brought forward from one year to the next within KS3. Freedom to Act is assessed as being in the upper reaches of *Directed* (E) (see Figure 12 and Figure 13).

The Impact of the job is advisory and supportive in the context of the management of the school. It is not a position shared with another, so Impact is assessed as *Contributory* (C) (see Figure 12).

The size of the school places it in the *Very Large* (6) category (see Figure 12), so the Accountability score is 304 (see Figure 15, Panel 4).

Example 3

Eastgate High School is a medium-sized all-girls Boarding and Day school, categorised as *Group 3* by the DfES. The job description stresses the importance of after-hours work: at lunchtime, in the evenings and at weekends. The position of deputy head is being evaluated using the Guide Charts. The duties for the post are as outlined on Figure 16, Panel 2.

> *Responsibility Analysis:* The discretionary component of the job is *Very Small* and the maximum time-span of discretion for the job's substantive tasks, as gauged from the job description, is *less than one month*. Duties such as deputising for the head, assisting in day-to-day administration, monitoring pupil absence, arranging staff cover and lunchtime supervision, have time-spans of discretion measured in days. The range of level of work is *Narrow* and a low Guide Chart score can be anticipated (see Figure 16, Panel 5).

> *Know-how:* The job, at its highest level of work, involves *Elementary Skills* (B), bordering on *Basic Understanding* (A) (see Figure 9 and Figure 10). The defined responsibilities merely follow standard school procedures and Scientific Know-how' is assessed as B-.
>
> The incumbent must frequently deputise for the head and the job is essentially one of being second-in-command. There is only one deputy in the school, so the Managerial Know-how is assessed as *Broad* (IV) and the Human Relations Skills at *Critical* (3) (see the two horizontal axes on Figure 9). If there is an error in this assessment, it is on the high side.
>
> Know-how is scored as 200 (see Figure 16, Panel 4).

> *Problem Solving:* The Thinking Environment is assessed as being in the lower end of *Routine* (B), confined as it is by standard school practice, with precedent and illustrative examples readily available in the small school. The job requires the incumbent to search for solutions within a fairly confined experiential area and to make discriminating choices between known things, so the Thinking Challenge is assessed as *Patterned* (2) (see Figure 11).
>
> Problem Solving is scored as 16%. It is a percentage of Know-how and 16% of 200 is 32 (see Figure 16, Panel 4).

PANEL 1

School:	Eastgate High School	**Ofsted:** January 2002
Type:	Girls 3-18 Boarding & Day	
Size:	400	**Group:** 3

Salary for job: See separate file
Equivalent positions: None
Membership of SMT: 3: H + DH + Director of Studies

PANEL 2

Position: Deputy Head
Duties mentioned in job description:
To deputise for the head.
To assist in the day-to-day running of the school.
To help with admissions.
To liaise with housemistresses in running the boarding section.
To monitor pupil absence and arrange staff cover for absent teachers.
To supervise lunchtime, after-school and weekend activities.
To coordinate special school events.
To assist with careers guidance and health education.
To assist in the appointment of staff.
To liaise with the head of the junior school to ensure a smooth transition into Year 7.

PANEL 3

Personal qualities required:
Commitment to the stated religious faith; be an inspiring (and experienced) teacher; be willing to take after-school activities.

PANEL 4

Guide Chart Analysis
Summary: To design, explore, develop, implement and support a whole school system for monitoring pupil progress.

Know-how:	B-; IV; 3		200	
Problem solving:	B-; 2	(16%)	32	
Accountability:	C; 3; S		66	**Total:** 298

PANEL 5

Responsibility Analysis
Discretionary element: Very small
Max time-span of discretion: Less than 1 month
Range of level of work: Narrow

Figure 16. Example 3 of a Guide Chart evaluation (Eastgate High School, Deputy Head)

Accountability: The job is one in which duties are subject to standard procedures and because of the short time-span of discretion, are closely monitored. Freedom to Act is assessed as being *Standardised* (C) (see Figure 12 and Figure 13).

The Impact of the job is assessed as *Shared* (S), since activities and resources are very much shared with the headteacher (see Figure 12).

The size of the school places it in the *Medium Small* (3) category (see Figure 12), so the Accountability score is 66 (see Figure 16, Panel 4).

The low evaluation score from the responsibility analysis and from the Guide Charts suggests that this position is not a management job at all, and should not require the appointment of someone at the level of deputy head.

SUMMARY

In schools, many job evaluations and classification procedures are outdated and inequitable. Confidence and credibility need to be restored to the pay and promotions system. At present, the same jobs under different titles are paid different rates, and different jobs under the same title are paid the same. There is insufficient monitoring of what jobs actually entail. The grading of jobs always depends to some extent on precedent and comparison, but recent media publicity suggests that equity within schools and within the teaching profession as a whole is being undermined by lethargy and the almost complete absence of analysis.

The goal of every headteacher is to have some rational means of ensuring that the right amount of financial capital, in the right proportions, is allocated to the right people for producing the right things. The Profile Guide Chart method is one such system. It is equitable from the point of view of recruitment and for the purposes of relating pay to performance. Similar methods are used in the commercial sector and are regarded as the industry standard. They conform to fair employment legislation and have been used in arbitration proceedings to indicate unfair treatment and determine job value (Jirasinghe & Lyons, 1996).

Admittedly, using job evaluation techniques in education is an attempt to rationalise the unknowable and the very existence of rationality in organisations is still a matter of some debate. Nevertheless, the approach has an inherent validity. If schools are rational places, insofar as any organisation is ever truly rational, then job evaluation is a legitimate tool; if they are not, if they are irrational 'garbage cans' as Cohen and March (1972 & 1986) would have it, then the process of job evaluation at least puts a veneer of manageability onto an otherwise random situation and the school is no worse off.

Job evaluation schemes can also stand as important symbols of change. They can be part of a wider, more visible, strategy for increasing efficiency. As best, the techniques are of proven validity and are rational, rigorous, objective and free of personal bias; at worst, they lack accuracy but must be preferable to the merely speculative.

Performance related appraisal is set to dominate the education agenda for some time to come, at least in the UK. If there is to be a realignment in the relationship between pay and responsibility for teachers and heads, and that seems inevitable, then better it is based on a transparent mechanism that rewards responsibility, than a system that feigns indifference.

CHAPTER 5

Pay and incentives in an education setting

> The individual has always had to struggle to keep from being overwhelmed by the tribe. If you try it, you will be lonely often, and sometimes frightened. But no price is too high to pay for the privilege of owning yourself.
>
> *Friedrich Nietzsche, 1844 – 1900.*

INTRODUCTION

Commercial companies have come under attack in the media recently for offering huge compensation packages to their executives; not so much the fixed salary part, but the ancillary components. In May 2003, for example, the shareholders of pharmaceutical giant GlaxoSmithKline rebelled over the remuneration package agreed with its chief executive; a regular salary of £2.4m and a 'golden parachute' of £22m. A week later, telecommunications provider Cable & Wireless announced plans to shed more than a quarter of its UK workforce, halt all dividend payments to shareholders and pull out of the US market as the full extent of the failure of the outgoing chief executive's period in office became known. The company made a record £6.5bn annual loss, spent £9bn over three years building a failed internet business (C&W Global), and in the year to the end of March 2003, made an operating loss of £303m on revenues of £1.7m. The outgoing chief executive received a performance bonus of £1.5m under his contract (Wray, 2003)!

Nowadays, the fixed component of salary for top managers is typically less than the incentive component, and in some well-publicised cases, massively so. And although shareholders and market analysts are concerned at the extent to which the use of incentives actually results in better management, ordinary employee pay has followed the same pattern, though naturally at a lower level of remuneration. Pay, commission, bonuses and employee share options are now increasingly tied less to length of service and more to output, and commentators have linked it in a causal way to increased productivity and decreased absenteeism (McKenzie & Lee, 1998). And consumers have been joined in the fray too, with extensive loyalty schemes creating incentives for customers across partnerships, such as that operated through the Nectar Card system by British Petroleum, Sainsbury, Barclays and Debenhams (see Chapter 2).

The use of incentives as components of pay continues to grow in importance because of the increased complexity of organisations. In schools, as in other service sector organisations, employees at the chalkface have know-how and expertise that managers do not - information about pupils, the curriculum and pedagogy, marking examination papers, and so on – and managers now rely more on this (the intellectual capital of employees) to maintain effective and efficient output. At the same time, increasingly they must be sure that employees are developing their intellectual capital with the interests of the organisation in mind, so there is an increasing tendency to use incentives as part of remuneration.

In the commercial sector too there is an increased need for performance related pay, caused at least in part by the fact that production and services have become globalised and more complex. Workforces can now be physically remote from management in a way that makes direct supervision by foremen impossible on a daily basis, and as a consequence, companies have had to become less hierarchical. Workers have had to be trusted to act in the interests of the company and the pace of change has meant that decision making has had to be devolved to lower levels within organisations. The old style 'command and control' is no longer an option for managers. The new style is one of enticement. Furthermore, for reasons of economy, companies have had to outsource many of their production and human resource inputs,[29] so there is sometimes an asymmetry between the business goals of purchasers and those of suppliers, which can only be rectified by incentivising the workforce at the production level.

Tying remuneration to objective measures of performance can cause productivity to rise substantially and can increase a company's market valuation (Aboud, 1990). Even the announcement that executive compensation is to be tied to performance can cause share value, which is a measure of investor confidence, to rise. Performance related inducement pay encourages risk-taking, whereas fixed salaries encourage risk-aversion, but as McKenzie and Lee and others have pointed out, the danger with incentive pay is that it can encourage short-term gain at the expense of long-term well-being. Managers can feel induced by performance pay to sacrifice higher long-term pay-offs in favour of smaller immediate pay-offs that ripen within the performance assessment period. Nowhere is this more evident than in the application of performance related pay to schools and universities, where academics, parents and teacher unions have documented a shift away from the traditional values of long-term learning towards short-term assessment success.[30] Despite government rhetoric,

---

[29] The manner in which sportswear manufacturer Nike outsourced its website management during the Sydney Olympics is a case in point.

[30] For example, many successful schools in England now oblige their students to do General Studies as a full A level, despite the fact that it is not accepted for entry at selecting (i.e. oversubscribed) universities. It virtually guarantees a high league table position based on the number of A level points per examination per candidate.

lifelong learning has been usurped by lifelong assessment where fixed dispassionate salary has been supplanted by short-term inducements.

In the commercial sector, short-termism is overcome by obliging managers to retain financial benefits like share options until a date well into the future, thus lengthening their time horizons. Something similar is needed in not-for-profit organisations like schools. Headteachers and promotees to middle management should, initially at least, be fixed into a medium-length contract, with safeguards of course, but still tied to performance.

Performance related incentive structures should be used with a certain amount of circumspection. It is important to avoid inadvertently generating *perverse incentives*; to avoid situations where employees are paid per fault since that creates an incentive to generate more faults. Incentives can have a negative effect if used in the wrong way or if incorrectly structured.

The best approach to incentivisation in the education sector is to involve everyone; national and local trustees, employees, parents, students and suppliers. It is not a zero sum game, as is generally thought, where one stakeholder's loss is another's gain (Kelly, 2003). It is a part-cooperative (mixed motive) game in which collegiality and individualism can both be nurtured to everyone's benefit. Inducement pay does not necessarily work in opposition to teamwork. Whereas commercial companies compete with each other by producing similar products or services at lower prices or supplied with greater convenience to the consumer, schools compete on the basis of matching service to expectation. Within reason, cost has nothing to do with it and although schools can make themselves friendlier, they cannot make themselves more convenient.

Not all schools service the same market, of course. Different schools cater for different expectations. England's leading private schools are comprehensive in terms of academic ability but selective in terms of wealth and social class, the leading state schools are selective in terms of academic ability but socially comprehensive, and the rest do the best they can with what remains. Leading private schools sell a product that prepares students to be confident 'public people' in a patristic sense. Typically, their students can look forward to inherited wealth, so escaping penury is not in their catalogue of measures of success. Leading state schools, on the other hand, provide a product that, for some students anyway, is the silver bullet that can slay the evils of poverty and ignorance. Different products for different markets; different incentives for different measures of success. It is crucial for managers to employ smart incentives and to understand them. For schools, this means employing different inducements in different sectors.

In theory, incentive schemes are necessary because the interests of employees do not always coincide with the interests of employers or those who represent the employer. Good incentives encourage reluctant colleagues to act not in their own selfish interests, but in the interest of the organisation. Management by diktat cannot carry the day anymore, even if employees still feel a sense of obligation to do what they are paid to do to the best of their abilities. As McKenzie and Lee (1998) have reckoned, incentives are simply a cheaper substitute for giving orders that would otherwise go unheeded.

Incentive schemes can also be used to reinforce objectives and strengthen an organisation's collective effort towards achieving them. They are, at a minimum, aids to good communication. Experience suggests that the dissemination of critical information by internal memoranda is not successful; importance and urgency are seldom communicated effectively and there is a certain perverse credibility to be gained among employees by ignoring them.

In communities of equally qualified professionals, like schools, the motivation generated by incentive schemes frees employees to use their specialist localised knowledge to overcome resistance to organisational aims; in other words, to reconcile the conflict between individual and collective interest. Without incentives and in the absence of command and control management, individual know-how cannot be properly coordinated to the benefit of both the organisation and the individual. The ideal is to operate a system of incentives that encourages employees to pursue their own selfish interests, but at the same time benefit the organisation and colleagues. The greater the perception of compatibility between individual and collective interest, the more desirable it is to have greater freedom for individuals. In a perfect world, employees would be given complete freedom to act in their own interests, and this would coincide fully with the collective organisational interest. In the real world, however, motivating teachers is a mixture of market incentivisation and government control, so full coincidence of motivation is impossible. But matching individual and organisation incentives is still an important aspiration; it points the way towards what is desirable.

The benefits accruing from incentives accumulate over time as incremental differentials are compounded. Incentive schemes can be the difference between success and failure, and although they are difficult to get right and no one size fits all, there are some underlying principles that should be adhered to. One of these is the desirability and importance of creating *residual claimants* out of employees in receipt of performance related pay; in other words, it is desirable that employees are given ownership rights to their own benefits, rather than given benefits-in-kind. Employees should receive benefit in a form that allows them ownership of it, otherwise there is no incentive to use resources sparingly or to reduce scrappage. If employees benefit from making good decisions, better decisions will be made. This is one of the difficulties with incentivisation in education; the system is underfunded to the extent that teachers cannot be made the beneficiaries of their own good decisions and headteachers cannot behave as residual claimants with their own budgets.

Incentives of course, need not be financial; simple politeness can go a long way towards encouraging more and better work from employees. No set of incentives, financial or other, is ever perfect, and this gives rise in the education sector to the question of *meta-incentives*; the incentive to find the right incentives for others. Currently, the system does not incentivise headteachers and local authority managers to find the best set of incentives for teachers.

PERFORMANCE RELATED PAY FOR TEACHERS: MORAL HAZARD, ADVERSE SELECTION AND PRINCIPAL-AGENT RESISTANCE

The introduction of performance related pay for teachers is intended to modernise the teaching profession by recruiting, retaining and promoting effective teachers, and raising the status of teachers in their own eyes and in the eyes of the public (Barber, 2001). It aims to create a culture in which teachers take prime responsibility for pupil performance and are rewarded accordingly. Traditionally, for cultural reasons, time-based seniority systems have predominated in schools and in public services, although

West (2001) has argued that it was the failure of managers properly to use existing mechanisms to reward performance and curtail advancement that was largely to blame for the system's ineffectiveness, rather than any inherent flaws in the theory. The old monolithic incremental pay scales, which afforded so few opportunities for advancement outside the mere fact of getting older, were never intended to provide automatic progression to the top of some notional ladder (Marsden, French & Kubo, 2000); it was simply that sanctions, where they existed, were rarely invoked by management (Megaw, 1982). It was not that the old seniority-based systems were inherently flawed; it was rather that they were badly managed, and in education, these cultural difficulties were compounded by a promotion structure that rewarded good teachers by taking them out of the classroom.

Whatever the relative importance of the various cultural and practical influences on the old time-based promotion system, it is likely that the introduction of performance related pay for teachers has been facilitated by the break-up of large bureaucracies like Local Education Authorities. School-specific performance targets are more easily set and appraised than nationwide or regional ones, though this in itself is not sufficient to overcome opposition to the ethos of individual self-interest that underpins performance related pay. Schools are subject to a tension in this respect: they are aware on the one hand of the need for team-based approaches to improvement, because research (Teddlie & Reynolds, 2000) and instinct suggest it makes for better schools, and on the other, a PRP-induced disposition towards individualism as a means of raising classroom performance.

The link between incentives and performance
When employees have significant discretion in the performance of their duties, the two main links between incentives and performance are the ability to recruit and retain effective workers, and motivation (see Figure 17).

Figure 17. The two main links between incentive and performance

These two parallel claims need to be examined in some detail in connection with inducement pay. Firstly, while in theory at least, performance related pay offers schools a greater opportunity to retain effective staff, its success depends on the extent to which experienced teachers are motivated by money to stay in schools they would otherwise leave.

Secondly, performance related pay purports to increase motivation among employees, although even in the commercial sector where performance bonuses have supplanted security and loyalty as the main motivation for recruitment, the veracity of that assertion has been questioned (Marsden, French & Kubo, 2000). But whether justified or not, the supposed link between performance related pay and motivation for teachers depends largely on the transferability of performance related pay's two supporting tenets to the not-for-profit sector: that of *moral hazard and adverse selection*; and that of *principal-agent resistance*. They are considered below, along with an outline of some theoretical assumptions about employee effort which must be made in order to sustain credibility in incentive systems in the education sector.

Performance related pay and motivation: Moral hazard and adverse selection
In any situation where payment is made by an organisation to an employee, labour and expertise are sold by the employee at some notional market value. Teaching is no exception. Properly qualified teachers sell their labour and expertise under a warrantee-type arrangement whereby their graduate status and pedagogic qualifications underwrite, initially at least, a certain minimum standard of performance.[31] While this reduces the incentive for teachers (the sellers of their labour and expertise) to act dishonestly, since they can be held accountable professionally, an environment in which performance bonuses constitute a significant element of pay simultaneously offers two distinct opportunities for schools (the buyers of the same labour and expertise) to act dishonestly:

- School authorities can unfairly withhold performance bonuses from teachers safe in the excuse that, since their labour is under 'warrantee', they can be blamed for not coming up to some arbitrary level of performance. Shifting criteria thus creates a *moral hazard* for the unfortunate teacher who, as with every warrantee, must rely on systemic restrictions to avoid spurious claims of failure against him or her. For an incentive system to function properly under such conditions of moral hazard, teachers need to be confident that they can rely on regulation for protection.
  The same restrictions on individual schools that are needed for the protection of teachers against the moral hazard have an additional beneficial effect: they serve to encourage honesty among schools *collectively*, for they know that if they act dishonestly towards teachers now, all schools in the future will have to pay higher performance related pay with more easily attainable assessment criteria. Collectively, therefore, schools have a rational incentive to act socially rather than selfishly, a situation analogous to the Prisoner's Dilemma in game theory (Kelly, 2003), and one that is considerably in teachers' favour.

- The second opportunity for schools to act dishonestly through an incentive pay scheme arises from the information imbalance. School managers have more useful information at their disposal about the pay-off structure than do teachers, especially if central or local government intervene, as they must, to complicate the system with limits and guidelines. Some schools may use obfuscation to set more difficult criteria than others, or they may demand more

---

[31] This warrantee arrangement works both ways of course - the reputation of teachers affects the reputation of the school – but it is usually the school that warrants the teacher and not the other way round.

work for a given bonus. If a local authority offers performance bonuses just equal to the pay for the average amount of extra work required to earn them, then only those schools who know that they will get more than the average amount of extra work from teachers will offer performance related pay at all. This amounts to a problem of *adverse selection*; only those teachers who estimate that they can earn their bonuses for an amount of work less than they would do anyway, benefit from it. An analogous situation exists in the commercial sector with warrantees. Some buyers are naturally harder on a product than others, without being downright abusive. If a seller or manufacturer offers a warrantee equal to the cost of the average repair bill, only those buyers who think they will be harder than average on the product will purchase the warrantee. Therefore, by definition, warrantees are always sold at a loss and if any attempt is made to increase the price, ever more reasonable users will drop out of the market. Only the worst users will find value in them. Inducement pay may therefore have the opposite effect to that which is intended. It may merely create a following of teachers who can achieve their targets and bonuses without doing what they perceive as additional work.

Performance related pay and motivation: Principal-agent resistance and school size
Incentive schemes exist in all sectors of the economy, though sometimes in latent forms. They are not confined to production companies. In schools, for example, inducements are generated by the prospect and process of advancement to headship, despite the impression being created, deliberately because of a naïve conceptualisation of professionalism, that educators just get on with the business of being as efficient as possible without the need to resort to vulgar inducement. This is a convenient simplification. On the one hand it ignores human psychology; on the other it contradicts the rationale for organisations existing at all.

Large organisations like local education authorities and schools exist because the cost of replacing their internally organised activities - cleaning, catering, administration, finance and accounting, and so on - with market-driven ones is higher or the delivery less stable. Large organisations benefit from economies of scale; that is, there are costs savings when all resource inputs (labour, resources and capital) are increased together and output increases by a correspondingly *greater* amount. In schools, when tasks are divided among a larger number of teachers along the lines of specialism, they become more efficient at what they do and can service more pupils in a given period of time. Effectively, large organisations substitute control for a type of free market exchange that would exist if everyone were driven solely by individual need (Coase, 1937).

However, large organisations cannot grow ever larger and expect economy-of-scale benefits to increase in line with the expansion. Firstly, larger organisations have more communication problems: the bureaucratic pyramid becomes depersonalised and individuals within it start to resent being directed only as part of a huge organisation. Entropy increases and consequently, employees must be offered bigger and better inducements to stay effective within the expanding structure.

Secondly, within larger organisations, conflicts of interest arise between certain identifiable groups. The goals of *principals*, who organise staff to pursue the interests of management, and those of *agents*, who deliver the outcomes, can sometimes be in direct conflict. Principals must get agents to work with the best interests of the principals in mind, and more frequently in large organisations, agents resist this and create a consequent *resistance cost*.

Thirdly, employees have more opportunity to shirk responsibility in larger organisations because their lack of contribution is less noticeable in the larger entity (Coase, 1988). It is not that workers become more dishonest; it is rather that their incentive deteriorates as the group expands (Olson, 1965; Isaac & Walker, 1988; McKenzie & Lee, 1998). Group size and individual effort are inversely related (Furnham, 1993), so to get the same amount of work from each agent, it becomes necessary for large organisations to offer incentives like performance related pay.

Economy-of-scale functions, which for schools depend on the nature and extent of the curriculum and pastoral service offered, are decreasing ones (see Figure 18). The extent to which size lowers individual teacher effort and increases communication and coordination costs, on the other hand, is an increasing function, influenced by the quality of leadership at the school and the extent to which staff feel ownership of the changes that have resulted from the expansion (Fullan, 1991). These two complimentary functions intersect at a point which indicates the optimal size of a school as an organisation. The perceived need for performance related pay in education suggests that schools may have exceeded their optimal size, though that size varies of course with context and situation.

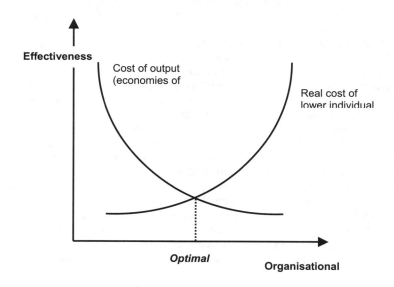

Figure 18. The optimal size of the school as an organisation

Performance related pay and motivation: Assumptions about employee effort
Performance related pay structures are underpinned by the assumption that low effort on the part of employees generally results in low output, and that employees by their nature wish to minimise the effort they give for any given reward. At first sight, this appears to be a not unreasonable assumption. If an employer offers a fixed low salary, employees will respond with low effort. The employer can then respond either by

lowering wages to match the low effort, or by linking pay to performance in the hope of encouraging greater effort. In either case, much depends on the ease with which performance can be measured.

Figure 19 shows the theoretical relationship between effort, output and pay in circumstances that allow performance to be easily measured. There is a perfect correlation between effort and output because they are perfectly measurable.

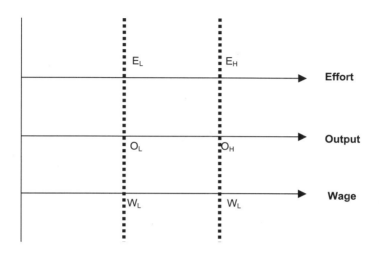

Figure 19. The theoretical relationship between effort, output and pay in circumstances that allow performance to be easily measured

Figure 20, by contrast, shows the situation when effort and output are neither perfectly correlated nor easily measured, which is the case with schools and teaching. For either low (E_L) or high effort (E_H), there is no precise known output, but rather a spread of likely outputs, represented by the boxes. These spreads overlap, showing that high effort (E_H) can sometimes result in low output (O_L), through lack of professional development, inefficient classroom management or lack of adequate teaching resources. And at other times, low effort (E_L) can result in high output (O_H) from students, as a result of compensation from home, grinds from other teachers or just good fortune. When the overlap of outputs is very large, high effort is almost as likely to result in low output as high output. So there is a significant chance that teacher commitment and hard work will go unrewarded, because high effort cannot be distinguished from low effort in terms of output.

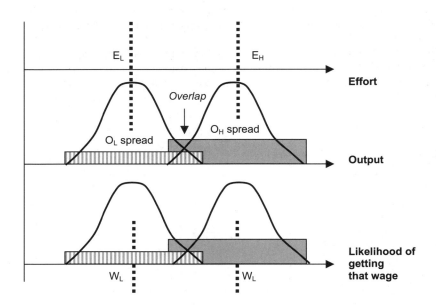

Figure 20. The theoretical relationship between effort, output and pay in circumstances where effort and output are neither perfectly correlated nor easily measured (the case with schools and teaching)

The ability to differentiate between levels of effort is critical to the process of performance appraisal and the perceived fairness of incentive systems. One way of doing this is to separate the output boxes on Figure 20 to the extent that they no longer overlap, or if they do, that they do so only to a very small extent. This *high gearing*, as the technique is known, must be large enough as a percentage of total pay to make for *distinguishability* (Lazear, 1998). In game theoretic terms: the pay-off must be made big enough to compensate for the chance that good work might go unrewarded (Marsden, French & Kubo, 2000).

A very good appraisal system can be an alternative to high gearing. It should have clear objectives, be capable of accurate measurement of outcomes and have transparent assessment criteria supported by a culture of responsibility. The search for such a system for schools is made all the more important by the impossibility of high gearing. Schools simply do not have the resources (or the freedom) to gear the performance element of teachers' pay highly enough. And yet, having a very good appraisal system is not enough in itself. Its application must be perceived by teachers as being fair. Research in the commercial sector has shown that performance related pay is sometimes regarded by employees as a device for cutting expenditure, that it is used to reward favoured employees, that management have quotas for recipients and that good work is not always rewarded (Marsden, French & Kubo, 2000; Milkovitch & Wigdor, 1991).

Similar feelings among teachers would be likely to impede rather than facilitate the introduction of incentive systems to schools. Not all of the assumptions that underpin incentive systems in the commercial sector translate well to education. Firstly, many graduates go into teaching for altruistic reasons and driven by a strong desire for independence. To that extent, they may resent it being assumed that relatively small performance related increments in pay would motivate them to greater effort. In addition, the principal-agent / moral hazard model of performance related pay assumes a Theory X view of work and workers (McGregor, 1960), but there is no evidence to suggest that this simplistic and somewhat outmoded view of labour represents reality any better than other models. The assumption that teachers are lazy and do the least amount of work they can get away with is not borne out by research, which suggests that a mixture of commitment to individual schools and individual children is enough to overcome any supposed tendency to sloth (Scott, Stone & Dinham, 2000).

Secondly, it is difficult to measure output in the education sector, except in the crudest sense, and it is even more difficult to link it in any causal way to input variables. What distinguishes teaching from manufacturing and other commercial service activities is the profusion and confusion of influences. In education, it is not axiomatic that low effort results in low output. There is, almost by the very nature of the endeavour, a large overlap between high and low performances, representing an area where, for a wide variety of reasons, high teacher effort results in low pupil achievement (and more rarely, the converse). In education, the variables are simply not controllable.

CONFLICT BETWEEN THE INDIVIDUAL AND THE COLLECTIVE

It could be said that moves towards greater accountability in schools is a manifestation of the fact that teachers are not trusted with conducting the business of education. It has resulted in a culture of compliance in schools and an expectation of surveillance within the teaching profession, but it would be a mistake to think that these phenomena are unique to education. In the commercial sector, there has always been a fear among shareholders that principals and agents could collude to exploit their position at the expense of shareholders. To reassure them, principals bond themselves voluntarily to shareholders' interests. They throw in their lot with them and in this way, shareholders are reassured to know that managers will suffer almost as much as they will if things go wrong. A potentially competitive situation is transformed into a cooperative one by declaration. The annual company report and trading statements are as much a benefit to managers in this respect as they are to shareholders; they reduce the opportunity for corruption, but more importantly, they reduce the suspicion of corruption among shareholders. That is why the market looks unfavourably on directors selling their holdings in listed companies; it removes the liability that managers would suffer alongside shareholders if things should go wrong.

Organisations generate cost savings through cooperation, but cooperation doesn't just happen, despite the moral obligation some people feel to do their best. Cooperation comes about largely as a result of inducements. Good incentives motivate individuals to act in the interest of the collective while at the same time being selfish, but sometimes the situation is complicated by conflict between individuals and between organisations. (Readers who wish for a deeper theoretical insight into this aspect of organisational theory are referred to the Appendix). Game theory suggests that incentivising cooperation is something that comes about of itself in situations where colleagues agree in advance to arrangements that punish those who choose non-cooperation. It is important that headteachers and school managers are able to identify game theoretic dilemmas (like those described in the Appendix) as they arise frequently enough within schools and between schools and external agencies. Schools that have evolved through cooperation are generally stronger because their teachers have developed an innate sense of belonging to something bigger than themselves, though they might still wish to work independently. This offers headteachers the potential to develop synergy, but it has to be harnessed carefully because ultimately employees cooperate most effectively when their own selfish interests are also being served. The trick for managers therefore is to arrange incentives so that this happy coincidence of interests comes about. The natural instinct is for personal survival and good incentives are those that cater to that instinct through the medium of cooperation with like-minded people.

PAYING EMPLOYEES ON THE BASIS OF OUTPUT

Incentives do not affect all forms of behaviour, but as a general principle, if employees are rewarded for doing something, they will do more of it, even if it is unsociable. For example, hotel and bar staff commanded outrageous wages for working on the eve of New Year, 2000. There is a rate of pay at which most people would work any time of the day or night, and managers have to find that level of remuneration and ensure that it is tied in some way to performance.

In theory, those who are self-employed have the perfect incentive scheme; they bear all the risk and reap all the benefits in line with the performance of the business, but this is a rare congruence (McKenzie & Lee, 1998). Usually, there is a difference between what managers want and what employees want, and the bigger the workforce, the greater that difference. In large organisations, employees are separated from managers by layers of bureaucracy, good communications are more difficult and the time between fault and discovery is longer. In addition, employees correctly perceive that as a proportion of overall output, their contribution is small and the opportunities for shirking are many. Supervision is more difficult and employees can exploit that, so managers must design and maintain appropriate incentive schemes to maintain productivity.

Some ways of incentivising employees involve money; others do not. Loyalty, trust and honour all have important roles to play in management, but they are sometimes insufficient in themselves to maintain employee commitment to the aims of the organisation. The simplest way of complementing these virtues is to make employees stakeholders in the organisation. As such, their reward is conditional on the success of the enterprise and therefore on their own output. The greater the output from workers collectively, the greater is each individual's pay.

Ideally then, it might appear that organisations should dispense with salaries altogether and instead pay piece-rate; that is to say, pay employees solely on the basis of production. In the case of teachers, this would mean payment by examination results or some similar measure of success. However, such piece-rate remuneration is fairly rare, even in sectors like sales and marketing where it is most easily applied. Most pay is tied simply to time, though of course all employment is contingent in some way on the economic success of an entire enterprise; if employees do not add to a company's output, they will eventually be made redundant.

There are many explanations why piece-rate pay is not more widely used. Firstly, the output of employees cannot always be reduced to pieces. In particular, it is difficult to objectively measure the output of workers like teachers, academics and administrators. Some would say it is difficult even to define their work. Secondly, while employees might be fully motivated towards organisational goals by piece-rate pay, the complexity of production processes today is such that there is no guarantee that this brings about an increase in actual output. In addition, it is likely that the complexity of these processes results in less than adequate job appraisal because so few managers can understand every aspect of every job, so there is uncertainty as to who exactly is to be held responsible for each outcome. At the end of the day, what gets assessed is what can be measured; everything else is ignored. And in jobs like teaching, that is pretty much everything.

Thirdly, if employees are paid solely on the basis of quantity produced, there is an incentive to sacrifice quality in order to increase production count. If teachers are paid on the number of grades A to C in GCSE examinations, say, there is little incentive for them to teach weak students or to teach anyone anything that is not examinable. This situation is further compounded by the fact that teachers, like employees in other sectors, are not always in control of the factors which affect their own output. It is not reasonable to pay (or refuse to pay) someone for something that is outside his or her sphere of influence.

When employees are paid a fixed salary, they are assured that their incomes will not be affected by the organisation's performance or by factors outside their control. When workers are paid piece-rate pay, they are being asked to assume a risk that may result in income variation, but for reward which on average will be higher than the corresponding fixed salary. However, for the piece-rate system to work in the organisation's favour, the hoped-for increase in employee productivity must exceed the premium that risk-averse workers demand, and this suggests a fourth reason why piece-rate pay is not more widespread: the premium that workers demand to compensate them for risk and variability is greater than the expected increase in productivity. There is nothing in it for the organisation; the employees are too risk-averse.

Piece-rate pay schemes are mostly found in organisations where the risk to employee pay security is perceived as relatively low in comparison to the potential benefit of increased productivity to the organisation; in other words, incentive pay schemes tend to be used where there no great variation in output is possible and where employees cannot easily be monitored and are more likely to shirk. Companies in the sales sector and small production firms are typical.

An organisation should not make employees responsible for variations in production that result from factors beyond their control. Being sensible about this can in itself result in increased productivity as a result of increased goodwill between management and workforce. Piece-rate pay systems should only be used when employers can make credible commitments to employees to abide by their agreements and not to cut the rate per piece when the desired increase in productivity is achieved. Unfortunately, both employees and managers have incentives to deviate from productivity agreements, and while such opportunistic behaviour is counter productive in the medium-to-long term, in the short-term it is another reason why incentive pay or piece-rate schemes are uncommon. In education, for example, it is reasonable to assume that as funds from central government become scarcer, headteachers will be forced to make the criteria by which performance related pay is awarded more demanding. If reward systems can be so easily abused by managers, employees will not sign up for them in future, even at reasonable premiums. The risk is perceived as too great because managers are unable to convince workers that they will not take advantage of them.

In some cases, piece-rate systems can have the opposite effect from that intended; they can reduce output as employees cut back on production. Employees are induced to lower productivity for the same rate of pay, rather than raise productivity for greater pay. It is important for managers to get incentives right and to be perceived as dependable in terms of sticking to agreements. Changing the terms and conditions of productivity agreements should only be attempted when the way of doing a particular job has fundamentally changed since the agreement was drawn up.

The unpopularity of the performance related element of teacher pay in the UK can be traced to something similar. The job has not changed significantly since previous pay and conditions agreements were made; yet at a stroke, the system of reward was altered. In fact, so blatant was this breach of procedure that the new pay system, which was due to be introduced in September 2000, had to be delayed two years because it failed to meet the legal obligation to engage in prior consultation (West, 2001). Thus it was that the paymaster - in this case the government acting on behalf of the state – came to be perceived by teacher unions as undependable, with the result that some teachers and heads lowered their levels of performance so that they now just meet the targets set for them and thereby preserve the option of achieving the following year's targets more easily. Clearly, these employees feel that any increased 'productivity' will be used against them in the future and that their employers will take advantage of them. Effectively, they have been induced to lower productivity.

Incentive pay for teachers in the UK has both a fixed salary component and a performance element. It is a compromise between fixed time-based salary and performance-based pay. Generally, such a compromise is beneficial to both employers and employees because both share the risks in a way that reflects the fact that output depends not just on the behaviour of employees, but on external factors as well. In education, for example, examination results in a subject do not just depend on an individual teacher's classroom performance, but on the whole-school performance of the head, the performance and expectations of colleagues in other subjects, the general ethos and discipline that pervades the school, and so on. Similarly, in commercial companies, production output depends not just on workers' efforts, but also on how much management advertises, the reputation of the company, the sales team selling the right products to the right people at the right time, and so on.

Employees and managers have a vested interest in having everyone in a company working together as a team, and have an interest in incentive pay as long as everyone else is paid similarly. To the extent than one employee's income depends on another's effort, employees only ever favour a pay system that includes an incentive element for everyone. The shortcoming of the performance pay system for teachers in the UK is the fact that the incentive element as a percentage of total pay is so small and therefore teachers cannot be sure that everyone else is working to maximise the benefit to all.

Although instinct suggests that some combination of fixed salary and performance incentive is most likely to maximise output and balance pay with security, no one proportion is suitable for all organisations because conditions of production vary so much across sectors and between organisations. Essentially, part-fixed and part-performance pay schemes - *combination* schemes - work because they align the interests of employees with those of the organisation *and* with other employees, without exposing either to excessive risk. And with the employer carrying some of the risk, employees can assume that the employer will work harder in their interests. As McKenzie and Lee (1998) put it, each party is motivated to contribute to the success of the other.

In the commercial sector, employees on pure performance pay earn more than those who are on fixed salary, to reflect the fact that they accept additional risk. Performance employees must be paid more because if both were paid the same, no one would take the riskier option. Even a cursory examination of performance related pay for teachers in the UK suggests that risk is something that is missing from the structure. Other than disappointment, there is no inherent risk for those who do not achieve at a high level. Almost all eligible teachers are awarded their 'threshold payments', so there is no sense in the profession of performance related employees getting higher reward for greater risk; everyone gets it anyway.

In some ways, the difference between salaried and performance-paid employees lies in the immediacy of their reward, which is contractual and short-term in the case of incentivised workers, and aspirational and long-term in the case of salaried workers. It is not that teachers on salary are not rewarded; it is that they are unsure of their reward (usually promotion) and there is no contractual obligation on employers to provide one. Incentive pay attracts a different type of employee, and this is the real aim of introducing performance related pay to education: it attracts risk-takers and aggressive producers. Workers who are driven to be more productive self-select into jobs with incentive pay, which has the additional desired effect of weeding out less productive colleagues. Headteachers know this instinctively. In fast-improving schools driven by outcomes, less successful teachers opt out of their own accord. Very few heads need to sack poor teachers. Usually they just leave, driven out in part by 'communication' from colleagues who are willing to commit to performance pay and able to survive and thrive on that basis, which is good news for better teachers, since it pushes up pay for good teachers because of the shortage of staff, and depresses pay for poor ones because of the surplus. However, on the deficit side, it makes poor schools worse as unmotivated teachers are driven to non-competitive schools to work for lower pay.

The problem for headteachers at schools where teachers are on performance related pay, is how to set challenging targets by getting teachers to reveal the full potential of their students when they know that that information can adversely affect performance criteria and remuneration. Common sense suggests that if there is a 'game to play', teachers will underestimate the innate potential of their students so as to preserve the greatest potential for exceeding targets in the future with the minimum of effort.

SUMMARY

Incentive pay in education is a complex issue. It is designed to attract a different type of recruit to teaching, and it does. Risk-takers and aggressive teachers self-select into jobs with incentive pay, which weeds out less productive colleagues. This in turn pushes up teacher pay for good teachers, but does little for under-achieving schools because unmotivated teachers are driven there to work for lower pay. Even in successfully competitive schools where teachers enjoy performance related pay, it is be difficult for headteachers to know the full potential of their students when teachers have such a strong incentive to underestimate it to preserve the potential for meeting future targets.

In the commercial sector, the fixed component of salary for top managers is now usually less than the incentive component, and ordinary employee pay has followed the same pattern, though at a lower level of remuneration. Pay, commission, bonuses and employee share options are increasingly tied to production and less to length of service. It is a development that has arisen from necessity: workforces have become more physically remote from management, which has made direct supervision impossible on a daily basis, and organisations have become less hierarchical. Workers have had to be trusted to act in the interests of the employer and decision making has consequently been devolved to lower levels. Tying remuneration to performance encourages risk-taking, but the downside is that it encourages short-term gain at the expense of long-term well-being and there is additionally the risk of inadvertently generating perverse incentives. Good incentives are those which encourage reluctant colleagues to act not in their own interest, but in the interest of the organisation. They reinforce objectives and strengthen the effort towards achieving them; if employees benefit from making good decisions, they will make more of them.

For teachers, the link between performance related pay and motivation depends largely on the principles of moral hazard and principal-agent resistance. In any situation where payment is made to teachers, labour and expertise are sold by them under a warrantee-type arrangement whereby their graduate status and pedagogic qualifications underwrite, initially at least, a certain minimum standard of performance. This offers opportunities for schools to act dishonestly, but these can be partly overcome by regulation.

Size is a factor too. Large organisations exist because the cost of replacing their internally organised activities with market-driven ones is higher or the delivery less stable. They benefit from economies of scale, but they cannot grow ever larger and expect these benefits to increase in line with the expansion: communications are more difficult and more costly, there is greater conflict between principals and agents, and employees have more opportunity to shirk responsibility. Increased size can lower effort and increase costs, and so have an opposing effect to incentive schemes.

In education, effort and output are not highly correlated and they are hard to measure. This makes performance related pay systems difficult to operate in schools. For any given effort, there is no precise known output; high effort sometimes results in low output and vice versa. Since effort cannot be distinguished high from low in terms of output, there is a significant chance that hard work will go unrewarded. And the complexity of teaching is such that there is no guarantee that an incentive system brings about an increase in the intended output of the school. If teachers are paid solely on the basis of quantity, there is an incentive, in theory at least, to sacrifice quality in order to increase output: teachers paid on the basis of grades have little incentive to teach weak students or to teach anything that is not examinable.

CHAPTER 6

The retention of intellectual capital: managing continuity

It is no good to try to stop knowledge from going forward. Ignorance is never better than knowledge.

Enrico Fermi, 1901 – 1954.

INTRODUCTION

Know-how is a form of organisational capital and preserving it within an organisation when personnel change is an important function of management. The most successful organisations in the commercial sector are the ones that retain knowledge when employees move to new pastures, and there is no reason to suppose that schools are any different in this respect. Having knowledge shared and valued widely within an organisation is key. It requires more than a good filing system; it is about retaining individual goals and corporate vision.

CONCEPTUALISING KNOWLEDGE CONTINUITY MANAGEMENT

Beazley, Boenisch and Harden (2002) conceptualised knowledge management as a pair of complementary processes: knowledge transfer *among current* employees and knowledge transfer *from current to successor* employees (see Figure 21). If there is a tendency to skew the way intellectual capital is managed, it is in respect of the relative importance given to these two synergistic processes. Traditionally, the transfer of knowledge among current employees has dominated the agenda and the potential know-how loss to an organisation when employees are replaced by newcomers has been largely ignored. The obvious consequence of this is that each successive generation of employee has to reinvent the operational and strategic knowledge base that previous generations took so long to construct. If the term *high leverage* is used to describe processes whereby a disproportionately high effect is generated by a relatively low effort, the deficit generated by employees leaving - a knowledge drain – can be said to create a culture of low leverage within an organisation. Intellectual capital is generated by the intelligent, repeated and refined use of experience. When an organisation cannot do that, it is the poorer for it.

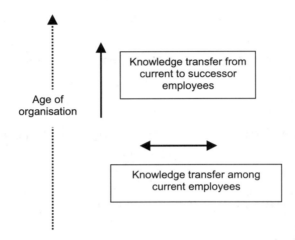

Figure 21. The conceptualisation of knowledge continuity management as a pair of complementary processes

Continuity management is about managing the second process; the transfer of knowledge from current to successor employees, between individuals who are or will be doing the same job. Frequently, a starting point is an organisation's *directory of expertise*, which typically emerges from an internal audit of expertise and craft know-how among staff. In large commercial companies, this can be posted on an intranet; in smaller organisations like schools, it is more likely to be located in the memory of the leadership team, which is not best practice. Better to have it codified and available to all than to risk its disappearance when senior managers leave.

Updating details of individual expertise should be the responsibility of individual employees rather than being the sole remit of a senior knowledge continuity manager. The updating should be regular, of course. In schools, it should be a contractual obligation rather than a professional need. It begins in a meeting of all employees engaged in similar work; subject teachers, heads of department, senior managers, careers advisors, and so on. These *peer incumbents* meet to codify the critical professional practices and know-how that they have accumulated over time, and which will in due course be transferred to the next generation of workers. It is simultaneously a knowledge transfer among current employees and a preparation for knowledge transfer to successor employees.

The need for knowledge continuity management in schools is driven by recent changes in the way schools are managed:

- Problems of recruitment and retention of teachers, even at headteacher level, has meant a high turnover of staff and a resultant knowledge gap between successive generations of teaching staff.
- Recent funding imperatives have resulted in schools replacing more experienced teachers with younger ones as a matter of strategy.
- The increasing importance of teaching assistants to the delivery of the education service has simultaneously lowered the fund of craft knowledge and made the transfer of it among teachers more critical.
- The demand (or perceived need) for continuous improvement and greater competition between schools has made the sharing of know-how more urgent but less frequent.

Of course, in any sector, as human resources become scarce and operational conditions become more difficult, tensions grow between the need to nourish the intellectual capital of individuals, equipping them to move onwards and upwards, and the need to tie that intellectual capital into the organisation. The solution is to codify all critical operational knowledge as soon as practicable, as if it is to be transferred immediately to successor employees. Having done that, it is then relatively easy to transfer it between existing employees. Craft knowledge with low leverage should not be transferred.

CHALLENGES TO KNOWLEDGE CONTINUITY

Organisational knowledge in schools resides in the thinking capital of teachers, management and support staff, and in the non-thinking internal capital of the organisation - its processes, routines, relationships, infrastructure, culture and symbolism. When they do occur, difficulties mostly arise as a result of discontinuities in the transfer of knowledge from one cohort to another, or from one generation to the next.

A break in thinking capital and the hoarding syndrome
A break in thinking capital occurs when most of the capital that pertains to a certain function is concentrated in a few people, and they leave the school. Such a concentration of know-how can come about as a result of management ineptitude, the school being too long in the comfort zone (where it is thought unlikely that anyone would even want to leave) or as is frequently the case with bureaucrats, employees refusing to share knowledge with colleagues because they perceive that retaining it exclusively makes them indispensable.[32]
Know-how dependency is, in the interim, very damaging to organisations like schools. Research undertaken for this book suggests that it occurs more frequently with deputy heads than with heads or teachers; more frequently among those with responsibility for timetabling and curriculum organisation, and less frequently among those charged with pastoral care. The most obvious way of dealing with know-how dependency is to convince incumbents of the need to share knowledge, or for managers to make it a contractual obligation to share and dismissing incumbents if

---

[32] It is perverse thinking because the more obvious the hoarding, the stronger is the imperative to get rid of the incumbent.

hoarding continues. A more pre-emptive and less drastic approach is for managers to rotate responsibilities among senior post-holders.

The effect of a receding locus of power
It is disconcerting when know-how exists in a school organisation, but no one is sure where it is. Organisational records may be incomplete or non-existent, or perhaps newcomers experience what Noble and Pym (1989) in another context have called the receding locus of power; the closer one perceives one is getting to the font of responsibility, the further away seems the prospect of getting a decision. At best, it is a waste of time on newcomers and their mentors; at worst, it remains as a disincentive a long time after the immediate source of knowledge has been located and tapped.

The problem of half-knowledge and lack of assurance
It is also disconcerting when *some* organisational knowledge is located, codified and capable of being shared, but is incomplete; significant chunks are missing. It is a half-knowledge, enough to keep newcomers frantic in their search for the missing pieces, but not enough to enable them to complete any task with satisfaction. Tasks are nonetheless completed, but not well enough that employees feel able to stand over their results with any great authority. They run scared that flawed recommendations will come back to haunt them.

The worst offenders in terms of passing on half-knowledge are those who themselves were victims of the same disadvantage. University academics and subject heads in schools are particularly prone to it, perhaps in a vain attempt to ensure that a successor is not successful enough to suggest a greater ability. In a sink or swim culture, no one is as impervious to struggle as the one just out of the water.

To be more charitable, it is all too easy for this kind of situation to arise in schools, where work is so often person-centred and success depends to such a large extent on imponderables like confidence in relationships, trust among stakeholders, and so on. Consequently, the problem of half-knowledge can and does occur in schools even when there is earnest good will on all sides, which makes the case for regular and structured knowledge continuity management even more pressing.

The need for knowledge, not witchcraft
Information overload comes about when newly qualified or newly promoted teachers are swamped with information, but do not have the experience or know-how to use it wisely to fulfil the school's objectives. The information may be wrongly organised (or not organised at all) or it may have been transferred to new staff without adequate explanation as to how it all fits together or how it should be used to attain certain desired outcomes. Information is not knowledge.

Alternatively, properly classified knowledge may have been properly transferred to incomers, but was out of date or just plain inaccurate. In the fast changing world of school administration, obsolescence comes about very quickly compared to other sectors. The shelf life for examination procedures, curriculum specifications, conditions of employment, performance appraisal criteria, careers information and so on, is very short and moves forward according to a political rather than an educational timetable.

Misinformation was once a tactic in times of conflict. Now the struggle to disentangle current from obsolete information is part and parcel of everyday life for educationists. Failure to do so - indeed anything less than total success – leads inevitably to myth and ignorance, guaranteed only to undermine good practice and reduce school improvement research to witchcraft. Success in preserving current know-how and encouraging a culture wherein it is sought-after and valued is best achieved through formal dissemination forums and critical reviews of understanding among staff and senior managers.

Changeability and the attenuation of know-how
There is a tendency, chiefly among those who have read but misunderstood Fullan (1991), to attach great importance to change for its own sake. There is now a self-perpetuating *changemeister* industry, peddling change when what is required is changeability. Knowledge continuity management is not concerned with change for change sake; it is about developing organisational flexibility in case change should be necessary. It promotes change that results in improvement, not change that merely results in difference. It is about evolution or revolution, depending on how good or bad the school is at the time, but never convolution. So part of the knowledge that should be passed from employee to employee, and from generation to generation, should be concerned with adaptability and the ability to innovate. Rather than wait until it is too late, schools, like commercial companies, should have *futures forums*, where change forces are recognised and the mechanisms for preparing for change are discussed. Newly arrived teachers and recently promoted managers need space to plan how their contributions are going to drive the school forward, and settled staff need to best-guess tomorrow's world: what will university entrance requirements look like in the future, what financial constraints are likely to operate, what is the future for a school-leaving exam at 16 if curriculum drivers are 14-19, how will changing demographics and recruitment problems affect post-compulsory curriculum provision, and so on.

Michael Fullan's great contribution to the change debate was his emphasis on the need for teachers to feel a shared sense of ownership of educational change, and the need to self-justify and incorporate new ways-of-doing into practice. At present, that happens too infrequently in schools, where teachers perceive themselves as passive recipients of educational change, rather than active participants in it. The result is *knowledge attenuation*, where know-how is dissipated throughout the organisation with the passage of time. The management of knowledge continuity aims to restrict that leakage and to retain as active as much knowledge about change as possible within the organisation.

THE BENEFITS OF KNOWLEDGE CONTINUITY MANAGEMENT

Knowledge continuity management accelerates the induction of new recruits and promotees. Fewer mistakes are made and decision making is better informed. In addition, in-service training can be tailored to individual need since there is greater certainty about what is required and what is not, which in turn results in better morale, lower stress levels and a 'longer burn' for employees. Knowledge continuity management ties know-how to the organisation through the individual, not to the individual through the organisation. It prevents knowledge hoarding and encourages information networking within an organisation. In education, knowledge continuity management can help overcome the twin ailments of recruitment and retention of good staff. It can reduce staff turnover, increase organisational effectiveness and build confidence in a school's systems. Every headteacher knows how unsettled parents and students get when key staff leave - they would be even more unsettled if they knew the actual extent of the knowledge gap usually left behind - so it is vital that there is widespread confidence in the school's systems; in other words, the school must be perceived to retain a memory of what it was that departing members of staff did that was so valuable. For example, knowledge about the needs of particular families and their pupils is critical to a school's effectiveness, so the requirement to maintain knowledge continuity or restore it as quickly as possible is paramount.

Accelerating the induction of newcomers
Continuity management allows a successor to pick up where a predecessor left off. The days when periods of grace were allowed for newcomers are over, largely as a result of the speed at which new economy commercial companies operate. While it is fashionable for some to talk of globalisation as the dominant feature of the new economy, it is a misconception. Since the development of reliable timepieces, which allowed longitude to be measured accurately and great distances to be navigated with certainty and safety, trade has been global. Trading in spices, sugar, tobacco, tea and precious metals was always global, as was insurance for the ships that carried them. Global trade has formed the backdrop to plays like Shakespeare's *Merchant of Venice* since Elizabethan times. There is nothing new about globalisation and it certainly isn't the result of advances in information technology. The salient features of the new economy are instead speed of access to information and the fact that information is no longer in the hands of the professional few. Craft knowledge used to be solely in the hands of professionals who sold their expertise in the marketplace, and the natural time difference that existed between markets meant that customers did not have access to professional information in real time. Only a few decades ago, for example, share traders in London and New York had to wait until the following day's newspapers hit the streets before they knew how the Nikkei market in Tokyo had performed. And in 1929, it took two days for news of the Wall Street crash to reach London. The new economy has certainly changed all that. All manner of specialist information is available on the worldwide web, and available to everyone in real time too. The new economy has made information less precious, more widely available and faster. It has abolished the buffers between sectors, between markets and between experts and consumers.
Where economics goes, education follows. Consumers of schooling now also have access to information (such as examination performance data) that was once the sole province of professionals and academics; and it is available in real time too. Information is now more in the hands of consumers. They want what they perceive as their entitlement; they want it now and they know immediately if they're not getting it. In a compliant society where the philosophical arguments about the desirability of making a market for education have been settled - if indeed they ever took place - schools cannot afford to have learners in teaching positions for a prolonged period of induction while pupils go without the most effective tutelage and confidence ebbs among stakeholders. Continuity management can help a school overcome this problem by shortening the period of initiation for new teachers and making it less disruptive. With continuity management, teachers acquire know-how more quickly, they learn the job on the job without it adversely affecting productivity, and ramp-up

time is reduced so that effective working is reached sooner.

Making a good initial impression
Initial impressions are important in retaining teachers at a school. Newcomers usually have reasonable career expectations and their initial perceptions of how quickly these expectations can be met has an influence on how long they are prepared to wait for fulfilment and the extent to which they are prepared to commit to the school. Good knowledge continuity management has the potential to encourage newcomers to imbibe (and contribute to) the culture and ethos of the school, and can shape employee attitude well into the future. It is an effective recruitment tool, attracting the best in the market to work there. The best newly qualified teachers want to get into their careers quickly and surely, meeting and sometimes exceeding expectations. Knowledge continuity management offers fast track employees a fast track start. To new arrivals, this is a manifestation of the school's commitment to its own future, while maintaining a concern for the welfare and success of its teachers, both of which are good for career advancement.

Knowledge continuity management integrates newcomers into existing networks of organisational support in the initial stages of their employment. Intellectual capital is generated through interactions, so human networks are important instruments in the transfer of know-how from generation to generation (Kelly, 2001). They aid the identification and acquisition of operational knowledge because every member has a multitude of organisational-neural connections. If members leave the organisation, the network has a memory of what they did and their know-how. Networks require continual maintenance, of course, but the alternative – no networks or having to restructure them every time someone leaves – is even more costly.

Improving and informing decision taking
The era of big decisions as a feature of management is past. Today is the era of small decisions, made at the front-line, whose cumulative effect determines the fortune of an organisation. It is a downward and outward drift in decision making which forces a larger number of employees to assume greater responsibility (Beazley, Boenisch & Harden, 2002). Organisations have thus become more responsive to their markets and better tuned to changing customer demands. Knowledge continuity management allows new recruits and promotees to operate better in such circumstances, reducing the number and significance of errors, building confidence and improving performance. New recruits have access to good information about past experience that can guide them in their decision making. If theory is the compilation of past experience, knowledge continuity management is theory operationalised; making continuous what is successful and codifying failure so that it can be avoided in the future.

Improving training
By comparing the know-how of employees who have just left, as recorded by an intellectual capital management team, with the know-how of their replacements, training can be targeted on shortcomings. This focused approach saves money and more importantly, saves time. It lessens the cost of the ineffectiveness that inevitably results from the unfocused induction of new employees. In schools, it avoids the

frustration, commonly felt among teachers during in-service training, which comes from being re-trained in what does not need to be done and in not addressing what does. Knowledge continuity management ensures that training is geared to the needs of the organisation and is motivating for the individual.

Removing ambiguity and building trust

Knowledge continuity management removes ambiguity by clarifying roles and abating the fear of failure that so often pervades the induction of new recruits and the immediate aftermath of promotion. It makes new recruits feel that they are valued and that their future contributions are viewed by management as being critical to the success of the organisation. The organisation shows its commitment to new employees by supporting the acquisition of know-how and making transparent the ways to get it. Reputation among colleagues, pupils and parents is very important to success in teaching. The confidence and competence build up as a result of good knowledge continuity management can be the difference between success and failure, between staying at the school and leaving after induction.

Reducing early job termination

Knowledge continuity management reduces the likelihood of early termination of contract by lessening frustration, confusion and stress among staff: teams last longer within the organisation and greater cohesion is encouraged; know-how, enthusiasm, morale and productivity are retained; a smooth transition is guaranteed to newcomers and existing employees alike, which is reassuring; the integrity of processes is maintained; job-turnover costs are lowered; and employees are guided to the most effective leverage strategies for improvement. Educators, more than most, know the importance of continuous improvement, which can only be achieved in learning organisations. Knowledge continuity management creates a learning organisation that continuously adapts or at least is prepared for adaptation. Stagnation comes about when organisations do not adapt or fail to see the strategic need to prepare for change.

Knowledge continuity management generates new knowledge every time existing know-how is transferred to other employees, because a new interpretation is imposed on it every time an incumbent operationalises what a predecessor did. Old insights are preserved and new ones generated when processes are described for someone unfamiliar with their provenance. And of course, newcomers replace experience with freshness, replenishing an organisation's potential for knowledge creation and challenging complacency. Knowledge continuity management allows organisations to celebrate the arrival of newcomers, by removing the fear of staff leaving. In fact, it could be said that continuity management is the antidote to organisational entropy – that winding-down malaise that seems to affect even the most successful schools as they age and is characterised by a lack of challenge to the institutionalised way of doing. Cages need to be rattled if an organisation is to prosper over the long term, and new recruits can do this most easily, or at least act as catalysts for existing incumbents to do it. Beazley, Boenisch and Harden (2002) put it thus:

> *"The objective of continuity management is not continuity of mediocrity but creation of excellence. It is from knowledge creation stimulated by the preservation of critical operation knowledge that innovation grows and*

excellence is achieved. Continuity management does not preserve the status quo, but challenges and changes it." (p.62).

<u>Easing dependency on external agencies</u>
Schools are forced to go where commercial companies choose to be; for example, outsourcing to knowledge contingency organisations. Reliance on outside suppliers like examination boards and teacher supply agencies potentially increases knowledge loss and ineffectiveness and poses a threat to the transfer of knowledge from one generation of employees to the next. Good knowledge continuity management allows a school to use outside suppliers without jeopardising its own intellectual capital, by capturing the operating know-how of outside suppliers and internalising it. Consequently, it is possible for a school to change suppliers or dispense with their services altogether – take the case of organising supply teachers, say - provided the school did not cede its expertise completely to external suppliers over the period of their use.

KNOWLEDGE CONTINUITY MANAGEMENT IN PRACTICE

Knowledge continuity management can be implemented at any level of an organisation and can involve any number of employees. The extent of the engagement is a function of the resources available. Ideally, knowledge continuity management in schools should involve as many staff as possible; the greater the number involved, the more likely the beneficial influence. However, no one size fits all and involvement will largely be determined by cost and benefit.

Any plan to introduce knowledge continuity management should be tailored to the particular needs of the school or sub-units within it. Thereafter, it should be easy to understand and implement, giving teachers and other knowledge employees the opportunity to codify their know-how with a view to transferring it to colleagues and successive generations. There should be immediate benefits for the transferor (the incumbent) and for the transferee (the successor employee). Primarily, this means giving an incentive to incumbents to continually update the knowledge management systems; successor employees already have an incentive in that their future professional well-being is dependent upon accepting knowledge transfer.

Updating a knowledge continuity management system should be made a contractual obligation, a basis for promotion and a feature of performance appraisal. Updating the knowledge continuity management system must be tied to an organisation's system of reward (or penalty) for incumbent employees. Departing colleagues are not always key supervisors - they are sometimes key subordinates - so it is in everyone's interests that knowledge continuity is taken seriously. Potentially, there must be something in it for everyone.

After a while, participation in and commitment to knowledge continuity becomes part of the culture of a school, so the imperative to have incentives diminishes as time passes. The priority then becomes one of maintenance. What management must do is ensure that there is no obstacle to participation and that associated bureaucratic chores are minimised.

Raising awareness and acceptance
The first step in any school knowledge continuity system is to get teachers to accept that there is knowledge leakage when incumbents leave and a new generation of staff arrive. Typically, management will have data on pending retirements so it should be able to demonstrate that staff turnover creates difficulties that are likely to continue unless continuity systems are put in place. The way to overcome knowledge leakage is to plan for it.

Teaching staff will be empathetic. Most know what it is like for a school to lose an experienced classroom assistant, laboratory technician, senior administrator or a good caretaker. The attitude among staff that knowledge leakage is inevitable is something to be dispelled. Knowledge leakage is not desirable and it isn't necessary, at least not on a significant scale, but it cannot be left to the last minute to plan the transfer of knowledge to successors. There must be school-wide acceptance that knowledge continuity can and needs to be managed, and there must be acceptance among senior managers that it needs to be resourced.

An unwanted legacy
When employees leave, they take with them operational know-how: timetabling expertise, local knowledge about families and pupils, how best to prepare for Ofsted inspections, how to manage relations with governors and local authorities, examination procedures, and so on. Yet all these operational functions still have to be performed, and the unfortunate successor faces a daunting prospect. It is daunting in a number of respects: the successor may be an unwilling inheritor who runs the risk of being perceived as incompetent following in the wake of a successful predecessor; it may be that the job takes a long period of familiarisation before confidence and competence can be built up; and the prospect of more unfamiliar administrative bureaucracy is disheartening, even to the point where potential successors leave as well.

Proper knowledge continuity management addresses all these concerns if it is implemented correctly. The key to success is nearly always to reduce the administrative overload on newcomers. Senior managers must reduce the fear of knowledge transfer among recipients, just as they must combat the inclination to hoard among givers.

Belief in the school's continuity systems is also critical. The only way to convince cynical teachers of the benefits to them (as well as to the school) of knowledge continuity management is to demonstrate in concrete terms how it would otherwise be worse: knowledge continuity management avoids duplication of effort, it avoids each succeeding generation having to rediscover what previous generations knew already, decision making is faster and better, it codifies experience, and makes promotion and performance appraisal a more attractive option for everyone.

SUMMARY

Professional knowledge is a type of organisational capital and preserving it within an organisation when personnel change is an important function of management. To preserve it within a school, there must be knowledge transfer among current employees and from current to successor employees. It is perverse to expect each successive generation of teachers to reinvent the operational and strategic knowledge base that previous generations took so long to construct.

Continuity management is primarily concerned with managing the transfer of knowledge from current to successor employees. A starting point is a directory of expertise, which typically emerges from an internal audit of craft know-how and begins with meetings of peer incumbents to codify the critical professional practices that have been developed and accumulated over time, and which will in time be transferred to the next generation of employees.

The need for continuity management in education has increased as a result of recruitment and retention problems, greater competition, and funding imperatives that have resulted in schools laying-off more experienced teachers. Additionally, the increased importance of teaching assistants to the delivery of the education service has lowered the fund of craft knowledge and made the transfer of it among teachers more important.

The organisational knowledge of schools resides in the thinking capital of its teachers, managers and support staff. Knowledge discontinuity occurs when most of the thinking capital that pertains to a certain function is concentrated in a few people and they leave. Such a concentration of know-how comes about as a result of a refusal to share knowledge because the culture dictates that retaining it exclusively renders the holder indispensable. The problem can be overcome by making it a contractual obligation to share know-how, and rotating responsibilities among post-holders.

Sometimes expertise and know-how are extant in a school's organisation, but no one is sure where it is because records are incomplete or non-existent. At other times, it is located, codified and capable of being shared, but it is incomplete. At the other extreme, newly arrived or newly promoted teachers can be swamped with information that is wrongly organised (or not organised at all) or has been transferred to them without adequate explanation as to how it fits together.

Knowledge continuity management aims to accelerate the induction of new staff and promotees so that decision making is better informed. In-service training can thus be tailored to meet individual need, which in turn results in a longer burn and a shorter ramp-up time for employees. Knowledge continuity management ties know-how to the organisation through the individual, prevents knowledge hoarding and encourages information networking within the organisation. It allows a successor to pick up where a predecessor left off, it can encourage a culture of cooperation in the organisation and be an effective recruitment tool by offering a promotion fast track for potential employees.

Human networks are important instruments in the transfer of know-how from generation to generation because intellectual capital is generated primarily through interactions. Networks integrate newcomers into existing structures of support, and aid the identification and acquisition of operational knowledge. Thus, confusion and stress among staff is reduced, greater cohesion is encouraged, and enthusiasm, morale and productivity are retained.

CHAPTER 7

Implementing a knowledge continuity initiative: an adjunct of lessons from practice

> There is nothing more difficult to take in hand, more perilous to conduct or more uncertain in its success than to take the lead in the introduction of a new order of things.
>
> *Niccolo Machiavelli (1469 - 1527), 'The Prince'.*

INTRODUCTION

Having developed a common understanding about continuity management among teaching and administration staff, the next step to establishing a knowledge continuity initiative in a school starts with doing a knowledge continuity audit and includes determining the extent of the initiative, setting up a post of responsibility for it and supporting its implementation. However, not all know-how is equally important as far as passing it to succeeding generations of employees is concerned. There must be some discrimination between the know-how that attaches to critical processes and that which attaches to other less important functions.

Critical processes are ones, which if done badly, result in the organisation failing to achieve its primary purpose. For example, in a retail organisation like a high street supermarket where the primary purpose is to sell for profit, critical processes include cash flow management, smart pricing and stock control. In educational institutions like schools, colleges and universities, critical processes are more varied and less easily defined because the primary purpose is more vague (see Figure 22).

Some critical processes: Pastoral	Some critical processes: Curriculum	Some critical processes: Administration & leadership
Staff consultation process	Staffing deployment	Policy-making process
Student & parent consultation	Timetabling: student liaison	Financial management
Discipline process	Timetabling: staff liaison	Distribution of funds
Careers guidance	Recruitment & redundancy	Promotion & appraisal
Personal & social guidance	Responding to change	Dissemination of information
Home-school liaison process	Quality control: teaching	Staff development
Complaints process	Quality control: learning	Industrial relations
External liaison process	Assessment of examinations	Ancillary services
Quality assurance of systems	Quality assurance of systems	Quality assurance of systems

Figure 22. Sample list of some critical processes for a school or college

Functional processes on the other hand are ones that are undertaken merely to fulfil legal or statutory obligations. They are the processes that preserve institutional life, but do not serve the higher purpose for which the institution was established. Functional processes are not properly the concern of knowledge continuity management: successor employees must fulfil them as a matter of course anyway and must personalise them in such a way as to meet their legal obligations. Figure 23 gives a sample of some functional processes in schools and colleges.

Some functional processes
Health & safety at work requirements
Fair employment practice
Contractual obligations
Reporting truancy & illegal activities
Keeping records of attendance
Ofsted / FEFC inspection processes
Keeping abreast of requirements
Financial auditing
Keeping records of attainment

Figure 23. Sample list of some functional processes for a school or college

Identifying critical processes (and afterwards listing the associated know-how that needs to be passed to successor employees) for some organisations is simply a matter of having a meeting or a series of meetings at the appropriate managerial level, but schools, colleges and universities consist of a plethora of independent working units within a complex collegium, and a widespread sense of the overall institutional mission is often missing. In order to focus on critical processes in such a compartmentalised environment, it is often desirable to get employees to prioritise the processes they perceive as critical within their own particular areas of responsibility.

Then some common school-wide form of scoring or weighting can be used to produce a prioritised list of critical competencies and know-how from different parts of the school. Figure 24 shows one such weighting system.

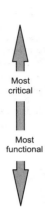

Type of critical process	Weight
Directly and immediately affects teaching & learning	100
Has indirect or delayed effect on teaching & learning	90
Directly affects student performance	80
Indirectly affects student performance	70
Directly affects teacher performance	60
Has indirect or delayed effect on teacher performance	50
Affects efficiency or provision of resources with direct immediate effect on classroom activity.	40
Affects efficiency or provision of resources with indirect or delayed effect on classroom activity.	30
Administrative processes	20
Functional processes	10

Most critical

Most functional

Figure 24. A sample weighting system

For every process that is identified as critical, an associated output should be identified. *Critical outputs* are what result from critical processes. They make knowledge continuity manifest and can be a means of gauging and locating knowledge discontinuities. By focusing on outputs rather than on processes, employees can identify how they contribute critically to the overall mission of the school. Most processes have a multitude of outputs, of course, so the aim should be to select a variety of representative quantitative and qualitative ones. Figure 25 shows some typical outputs for some typical critical processes.

Scoring individual processes in this way focuses attention on critical processes and hence on the critical know-how that needs to be passed to successors. Of course, it is possible, in theory at least, to look at every process in a school as critical in some respect and this would undoubtedly be a more rigorous approach. But in the real world, where resources are finite and time valuable, it is unlikely that the extra expenditure would make a commensurate difference to the quality of the continuity management initiative.

Critical processes	Some critical outputs
Staff consultation process	Staff morale & professional satisfaction
Student & parent consultation	Confidence & awareness
Discipline process	Exclusion & suspension rates
Careers guidance	Employment & progression rates
Personal & social guidance	Customer confidence & awareness
Home-school liaison process	Retention rates
Complaints process	Time in disputes & customer satisfaction
External liaison process	Community & business involvement
Staffing deployment	Staff & subject comparisons
Timetabling: student liaison	Customer satisfaction
Timetabling: staff liaison	Staff morale & professional satisfaction
Recruitment & redundancy	Staff turnover rates
Responding to change	Confidence
Quality control: teaching	Competence
Quality control: learning	Competence
Assessment of examinations	Comparison of examination results
Quality assurance of systems	Efficiency & effectiveness comparisons
Policy-making process	Professional satisfaction & awareness
Financial management	Per capita & nature of expenditure
Distribution of funds	Per capita & nature of expenditure
Promotion & appraisal	Staff morale & internal promotion rates
Dissemination of information	Awareness
Staff development	Attendance of staff at courses
Industrial relations	Time lost through disputes
Ancillary services	Resources used to support teaching

Figure 25. Critical processes and some critical outputs

PRIORITISING CRITICAL PROCESSES

Having gathered together the critical processes from each division of a school, the next step is to agree a list of the most urgent ones, without regard to managerial division, but with as much consensus and consistency as possible. Since tables of critical processes are compiled from prioritised lists, they can be customised for each school so that important staff departures are dealt with immediately. Each school's *urgency list* (Figure 26 shows a sample) will be different, depending on circumstances and organisational maturity, but in all cases, when the most urgent staff departures are catered for, other critical processes and their operatives take their turn in the queue. Knowledge continuity management is a continuous process, not a fixed outcome.

Urgent critical processes	Weight	Suggested outputs
Discipline process	90	Measurement of exclusion and suspension rates. Measurement of student, teacher and parent satisfaction. Measurement of student, teacher and parent awareness.
Quality control of teaching	100	Measurement of attendance, punctuality, examination achievement etc. Data from peer assessment and sharing experience. Measurement of student and teacher self-perception.
Examination analysis	50	Analysis of results, subject by subject, in relation to national averages and Year 7 intake (SATs etc). Measurement of progression rates to employment, further & higher education. Measurement of teacher & student satisfaction.
Home school liaison	70	Measurement of retention and truancy rates. Measurement of quantity and nature of complaints. Measurement of parent & teacher satisfaction.
Staff development	60	Measurement of attendance at professional development courses. Measurement of time and resources spent on professional development. Measurement of teacher satisfaction.

Figure 26. A sample urgency list

Since the framework for scoring the relative importance of critical processes that individual employees undertake is so crucial, it is often a contentious and emotionally charged issue. In a school or college setting, it is most likely to affect deputy heads, vice-principals and middle line managers. A sensitive, empathetic, approach by a knowledge continuity team is likely to pay dividends in the long run, particularly if any discontinuity is due to ignorance rather than incompetence.

Scoring the relative importance of different critical processes and the know-how associated with them is important. While simple weighting is one method of prioritising processes, another is to survey staff opinion using complementary *scorecards*. One scorecard measures the *strategic importance* of each process (see Figure 27) and the other measures the *ease* with which teachers think knowledge about it can be passed from one incumbent to another (see Figure 28). The scores for Ease and Importance are then plotted as a coordinate pair on a grid like the one shown on Figure 29. The scale on the axes can be adjusted to accommodate the range of responses obtained from the scorecards (Gurbaxani & Whang, 1991; Kelly, 2001).

SCORECARD **IMPORTANCE**		Name: Date:		
Critical process	**Max score**	**Actual score**	**Weight**	**Weighted score** Range = 0 - 100
Staff consultation	10		5	
Student & parent consultation	10		7	
Discipline & rewards system	10		10	
Careers guidance	10		9	
Personal & social guidance	10		9	
Home-school liaison system	10		7	
Complaints procedure	10		7	
External liaison system	10		7	
Quality assurance	10		7	
Staffing deployment	10		10	
Timetabling: liaison with students	10		10	
Timetabling: liaison with staff	10		10	
Redundancy & recruitment of staff	10		7	
Staff induction	10		5	
Ability to respond to change	10		6	
Quality control: teaching	10		10	
Quality control: learning	10		10	
Prediction of attainment	10		3	
Policy-making process	10		3	
Financial management	10		4	
Internal distribution of funds	10		7	
Promotion & appraisal of staff	10		5	
Dissemination of information	10		5	
Staff development & training	10		6	
Industrial relations	10		6	
Ancillary services	10		2	

Figure 27. Sample staff scorecard: Importance of a sample of critical processes

SCORECARD **EASE WITH WHICH KNOW-HOW CAN BE PASSED TO SUCCESSOR** 1 = very hard to pass on 5 = very easy to pass on	Name: Date: Please circle						
Critical process	**Actual score**					Weight	Weighted score
	Hard				Easy		Range = 0 - 50
Staff consultation	1	2	3	4	5	5	
Student & parent consultation	1	2	3	4	5	7	
Discipline & rewards system	1	2	3	4	5	10	
Careers guidance	1	2	3	4	5	9	
Personal & social guidance	1	2	3	4	5	9	
Home-school liaison system	1	2	3	4	5	7	
Complaints procedure	1	2	3	4	5	7	
External liaison system	1	2	3	4	5	7	
Quality assurance	1	2	3	4	5	7	
Staffing deployment	1	2	3	4	5	10	
Timetabling: liaison with students	1	2	3	4	5	10	
Timetabling: liaison with staff	1	2	3	4	5	10	
Redundancy & recruitment of staff	1	2	3	4	5	7	
Staff induction	1	2	3	4	5	5	
Ability to respond to change	1	2	3	4	5	6	
Quality control: teaching	1	2	3	4	5	10	
Quality control: learning	1	2	3	4	5	10	
Prediction of attainment	1	2	3	4	5	3	
Policy-making process	1	2	3	4	5	3	
Financial management	1	2	3	4	5	4	
Internal distribution of funds	1	2	3	4	5	7	
Promotion & appraisal of staff	1	2	3	4	5	5	
Dissemination of information	1	2	3	4	5	5	
Staff development & training	1	2	3	4	5	6	
Industrial relations	1	2	3	4	5	6	
Ancillary services	1	2	3	4	5	2	

Figure 28. Sample staff scorecard: Ease with which know-how about a sample of critical processes can be passed to a successor

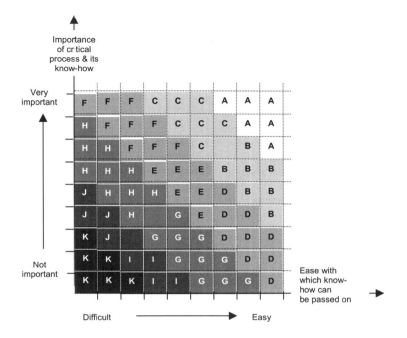

Figure 29. Grid for prioritising critical processes

Obviously, the ideal situation is to initially select processes whose know-how is easily passed to successors and which are very important to the organisation's effectiveness - Squares A on Figure 29. Other high scores come from critical processes whose know-how is easy to pass on, but which are not very important - Squares B & D on Figure 29 - and from processes whose know-how is difficult to pass on, but which are very important - Squares C & F on Figure 29. The situations become less favourable as one goes towards Squares K, where the processes have know-how that is difficult to pass to successors and are of little (relative) importance.

The order in which a school chooses to deal with the retention of its critical process know-how depends on how desperate the school is for improvement, although clearly, all other things being equal, critical processes in Squares A should be done first. If improvement is needed urgently, a school should move in the order ACFBEH....., seeking out the processes that have high potential, irrespective of how difficult the know-how is to pass on. If, on the other hand, it is more important to the organisation (and to staff morale, say) that some know-how retention is achieved, no matter how small, then the school should follow the path ABDCEG....., seeking out process know-how which is easy to pass on, irrespective of potential saving. The mixed option is to follow the order ABCDEF....., balancing risk and potential.

Knowledge continuity management is a long and continuous process so it is important to have as many people on-board as possible. Whatever steps need to be taken to ensure that this is the case should be taken. Self-examination plays a vital role, so preliminary work sometimes has to be done to create the right climate for professional reflection in the school. Organisational priorities change over time, as does the critical process know-how, so reflection has to be both critical and continuous. It is best if teachers take ownership of that reflection process and undertake participation with a sense of security and self-determination.

MAPPING CRITICAL PROCESSES

After a list of prioritised critical processes has been compiled, urgent processes must be examined in greater detail in order to understand the intricacies of what members of staff do to fulfil their functions within the organisation. What people do and what they say they do are not necessary the same and it is often a good idea to represent the internal workings of each critical process on a diagram. This is known as *mapping* the critical processes and an example is set out on Figure 30.

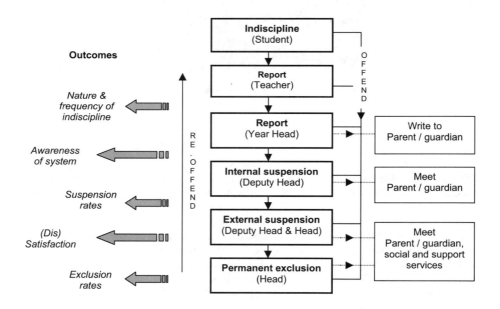

Figure 30. An example (Discipline) of an internal map of a critical process and its know-how

Maps should be shown to participating staff and agreed with them as part of the knowledge continuity management process. It reassures staff and helps to ensure that critical processes are accurately represented and that the continuity planners know what know-how has to be transferred, from whom and to whom.

Many successful schools and colleges have similar critical processes and follow a similar pattern. What makes one institution different from another is the way in which its critical processes are internally structured and how they interact with one another. This is why successful knowledge continuity management needs both a macroscopic and a microscopic view. The latter is got from understanding the detailed internal workings of the various critical processes and the former is got from putting the processes together so that they form a coherent representation of the organisational whole.

THE KNOWLEDGE CONTINUITY AUDIT AND IMPLEMENTING A CONTINUITY INITIATIVE

It is easier to identify where potential knowledge discontinuities might occur than to plan for knowledge continuity in the abstract. Pending retirements and such like are known in advance to managers and the need for knowledge transfer to successors can be planned fairly easily if the critical processes have been mapped. However, the risk from unplanned (non-retirement) departures is more difficult to handle. The best strategy is to audit every employee, beginning with the most obviously important and working downwards in respect of the complexity of the knowledge the employee would leave behind and the disruptiveness that would be caused if that knowledge were not transferred to successors. Granted, some knowledge is simply too complex to pass on in a meaningful way to successors, and not all knowledge is equally important, but that analysis is best made *after* an audit.

The jobs for which critical process know-how needs to be captured and transferred to successors should be listed. So too should the extent to which the know-how is technical and the extent to which the school's culture and reward systems are aligned to support it (Beazley, Boenisch & Harden, 2002). In commercial companies, it is possible to confine knowledge continuity management to the top echelons of an organisation; to departing and succeeding chief executives for example, where a successor-designate is usually in position long before the departure of an incumbent. But this is not the case in schools, where departures are less predictable and there are insufficient resources to support manager-designate positions for a protracted period of time.

The extent to which distributed leadership is a feature of management in education suggests that knowledge continuity management in schools and colleges should include virtually every professional employee. Initially, however, it may be wise to confine knowledge continuity initiatives to departments or divisions within a school, like Pastoral Care or Modern Languages, for example. The advantage of a piecemeal approach is that an audit can thereby be confined to cover only the relevant range and detail; the disadvantage is that the synergies (Beazley, Boenisch & Harden, 2002) that result from organisation-wide knowledge continuity are lost and the reward for the school is correspondingly diminished. Research suggests that piecemeal knowledge continuity procedures rarely become integrated into the day-to-day management of an organisation and are seldom supported by an organisation's system of rewards. And in schools, if the number of teachers participating in a continuity initiative is small, there is a greater likelihood that know-how will be lost. A confined continuity initiative means fewer resources to capture and transfer know-how.

Clearly, within each job there are varying complexities of competence and know-how, and differing levels of operating expertise. Knowledge continuity management is about recognising the critical components within that array and transferring the associated competencies and knowledge to successors. The difficult part, in practice, is knowing what is important enough to include and what is trivial enough to exclude, erring on the side of inclusion despite the obvious cost implications.

THE VALUE OF NETWORKS AND TEAM-WORKING TO KNOWLEDGE CONTINUITY MANAGEMENT

Someone, usually a deputy head or a head of department, has to assume responsibility for coordinating the management of knowledge continuity in a school. It will depend on the extent of the proposed implementation. If it is confined to one department, it is appropriate for a curriculum (middle) manager to lead the initiative; if it is a school-wide initiative, perhaps someone more senior; if it is wider still, say across a local education authority, then someone who has seniority and credibility outside and between schools should lead the initiative. A formal arrangement, rather than an ad hoc understanding, is recommended. The coordinating post is not likely to be too onerous over the long term, but it is likely to be time-consuming in the short term. Much depends on the resources allocated to the initiative at the start. If good systems are set up within the school, knowledge continuity eventually becomes part of everyone's *modus operandi* and the expectation becomes part of the organisational culture.

Knowledge continuity management cannot be imposed by diktat. It requires the cooperation of staff, so an essential ingredient to success is the extent to which a coordinator can build effective teams around the issues thrown up by the prospect of knowledge discontinuity. Knowledge continuity management necessarily involves the coming together of individuals or groups of individuals from within a school and the manner in which they form a network is of obvious importance.
A network is an intermeshed system of information conduits involving individuals or groups of individuals working together towards a common goal. The networked system links together factions that have common interests, enabling them to share resources, ideas and experience in an efficient manner. The complexity of networks varies of course, but they all aspire to add intelligence value to the knowledge continuity services they are charged with providing and retaining.
From an organisational point of view, intelligence is the ability of a school to learn and is a measure of its quickness to take meaning from experience. It is the getting and distribution of know-how and competence that informs the school's purpose. There are two features of organisational intelligence in particular that make networked organisations different from non-networked ones, and that have a bearing on the management of intellectual capital: where the intelligence (experience and memory) of the organisation resides; and how the fluidity of its members' efforts affects its effectiveness.

The partition of intelligence in networks
Network intelligence is the ability of a network to accumulate, share, adapt and distribute information gained from experience. It imparts value to the remedial actions

a school decides to take in its attempt to manage intellectual capital and knowledge continuity. The conduits which distribute this information can be *passive* or *active*; in other words, they can simply transport information or they can additionally interpret and add value to it. Active networks add value because they enhance passing information and retain a memory of it. Where intelligence resides, so too does the ability to add and retain value. If no network exists, intelligence is static. Value can only be added where intelligence lives.

Some writers (Sawhney & Parikh, 2001) have differentiated between *back-end* and *front-end* organisational intelligence. The former is intelligence that becomes embedded in the shared infrastructure of a network core; it is centralised, robust and standardised. The latter, on the other hand, fragments into different forms at the periphery of a network; it is decentralised, flexible and contextualised. The type of intelligence needed by a school managing its intellectual capital is back-end intelligence; the need and ability to store and process institutional memory. This is very different from the front-end intelligence a school needs to handle its dealings with students and parents at the customer interface (Kelly, 2001). If more than one kind of intelligence is required at any given place at any given time, then they may need to be coupled together artificially. But with that exception, a school network needs to partition its two intelligences so that the core can efficiently store and process information and the periphery can be customised to meet the requirements of individual teachers. Unnecessary duplication must be avoided.

The *partition of intelligence* is one determinant of a network's efficiency. In an efficient network, back-end intelligence is not replicated at peripheral points. It is pushed back to the core, where it is embedded in the infrastructure of the network. Meanwhile, front-end intelligence is deliberately fragmented at the periphery of the network, and the conduits between the periphery and the core are hollowed out to become passive, with little or no capacity for adding value themselves (Sawhney & Parikh, 2001). Only the peripheral ends and the core become significant sources of value creation and retention (see Figure 31).

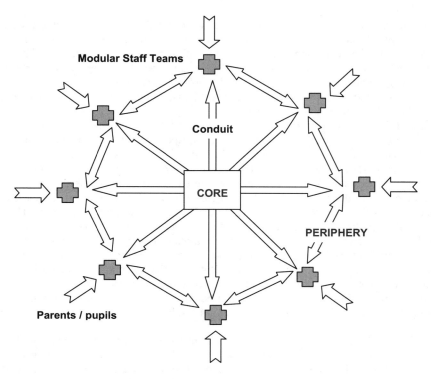

Figure 31. A networked organisation

<u>The fluidity of effort in networks</u>
The effort of a network is the sum of the individual attempts to achieve its objectives, and the fluidity of this effort – how easily it can respond to new organisational demands - is another determinant of its effectiveness. It reflects the way a school organises its staff and its stakeholders, and the way it serves the local community.

In traditional school organisations and universities, individual teachers are tightly grouped in large units of effort, isolated from each other in departments or faculties, in a crystalline structure (see Figure 32). In contrast, a modern networked organisation has small free-floating units of effort which coalesce into temporary coalitions whenever and wherever they need to; a networked organisation is fluid (see Figure 33).

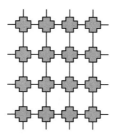

Figure 32. A traditional (tightly grouped) organisational structure

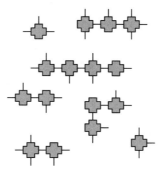

Figure 33. A modern (flexible) organisational structure

This notion of *fluidity of effort* has profound implications for an organisation, such as a school, in pursuit of intellectual capital management. Different individuals or groups of individuals can combine their capabilities and resources in temporary and flexible alliances to capitalise on particular opportunities or to address particular issues. Management then becomes primarily concerned with orchestrating and co-ordinating effort and the flow of intelligence, rather than with instructional leadership. It must facilitate the development of a common protocol for exchanging information and experience, without which individual coalitions would not be able to communicate with each other, never mind collaborate. Management must ensure that staff development programmes address this need (see Figure 34).

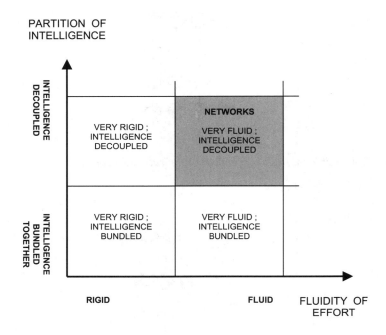

Figure 34. The partition of intelligence and fluidity of effort

The changing location of value
Schools preparing for intellectual capital management or consolidating their
knowledge continuity initiatives must take account of the influence of 'partition' and
'fluidity' on their structures. Modern organisations need to be highly connected
internally to be able to respond to change. For schools, colleges and universities, the
ability to respond to student (and external) demands is now more important than the
ability to simply teach or do. The notion of adding and retaining value has altered too.
In a network, everyone and everything is connected and value behaves differently
than in a traditional hierarchical organisation:

Value added at the ends and retained in the core: Most added value is created at the
periphery, near the customer, where highly customised connections are made.
However, as far as managing intellectual capital and knowledge continuity is
concerned, the important thing is that the value generated by interactions at the
periphery is retained at the core, where generic data-gathering functions consolidate
know-how and competencies.

Value in a common infrastructure: Schools committed to managing intellectual
capital and knowledge continuity should be networked organisations, in which
elements of infrastructure that were once distributed among different departmental
units are brought together and operated as a loose singularity. This shared
infrastructure typically takes the form of basic experiential storage-type functions as

well as common business-type functions like administration, timetabling, marketing and home-school liaison.

Value in modularity: In a network, organisational capabilities and processes are restructured as well-defined, self-contained modules which can quickly and seamlessly connect together. If a value-adding / value-retaining process is conceptualised as a series of modules operating sequentially to create a process by which some piece of intelligence has value added to it and is retained by the organisation, then success in knowledge continuity management lies in creating modules that can be plugged into as many different value-adding / value-retaining processes as possible so that organisational capability can be distributed as broadly as possible (see Figure 35).

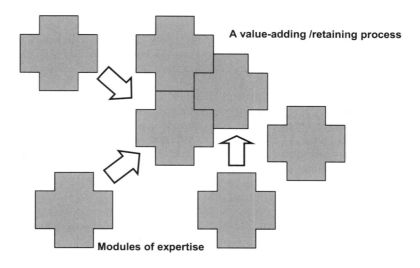

Figure 35. The value in modularity: modules that can be plugged into a variety of value-adding / value retaining processes

Value in orchestration: As modularisation within organisations becomes more prevalent, the ability to coordinate independent modules becomes a valuable new leadership skill, and has to be part of any management strategy for knowledge continuity and intellectual capital retention.

RESHAPING AN ORGANISATION AS A NETWORK OF TEAMS

The shrinking of middle management in schools is a consequence of what can be termed the *pacification of network conduits*, as intelligence gets pushed both to the core (senior management team) and to the periphery (reception staff and teachers). Networked organisations have less need for middle managers because communication is faster and easier, and collaboration almost unwitting. In old style organisations, before communication became what it is today, middle managers were needed to package and distribute information on its way up and down the organisational structure between the core and the periphery. This *information-sorting* function of middle (departmental) management is now redundant in schools committed to preserving intellectual capital. Such schools have passive pipework and the role of middle management, where it exists at all, is to facilitate direct communication between the core and the periphery so that know-how can be memorised.

Just as value-adding intelligence is now concentrated at the periphery of a network, value-retention and functionality is located more at the core. In schools, leadership and strategic functions are concentrated in a core of senior management, and day-to-day decision making functions are pushed to the teaching periphery, creating the need for a new professionalism among teachers.

Fluidity of effort is having its effect too. Organisational capability has become more distributed and modular. Passive conduits allow dispersed individuals to connect together to solve problems and respond to opportunities as and when they arise, without cost to the organisation. Cooperation between previously unconnected departments is no longer problematic or unusual; in fact, it has become an expectation. In schools, parents and students expect access to coherent information from any and every part of the organisation through web sites and intranet facilities. It is no longer acceptable to shunt parents from one department to another, claiming lack of jurisdiction. Networks allow access to information to become increasingly remote and free, and while such fundamental restructuring of a school and the professions within it is threatening, it does offer certain opportunities:

- Parents and students can become better informed and therefore (potentially) more supportive.
- Competing schools can come together more freely to provide a better public service, safe in the knowledge that engagement and disengagement are easily effected.
- Since communication is more efficient and immediate, the depository for intellectual capital can be located anywhere within a school's network. It can be moved to a new site as required to take advantage of or cater for a deficiency in expertise or experience.

The greatest obstacle to restructuring a school as a networked organisation dedicated to saving its intellectual capital is the preconception of what the result should look like. Schools reconfigured as *intellectual capital aware* need properly trained managers who have the confidence to overcome preconceptions. The need to understand the nature of organisational networks means that senior managers must dedicate resources to both the knowledge continuity core and the teaching periphery, and they must support the value-retaining and value-adding processes that take place (respectively) in both places. Middle managers must change their role from *filtration* (sorting information as it passes up and down the organisation) to *facilitation* (orchestrating the interaction between the players at the periphery and the managers at the core). Organisational elements at the periphery, where the school interfaces with its external stakeholders, must accept more responsibility and self-direction. Action must be predicated on independent judgement and informed by institutional strategy (see Figure 36).

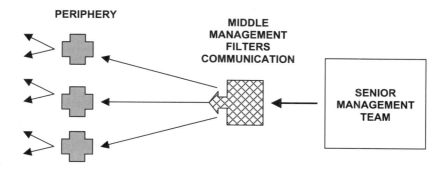

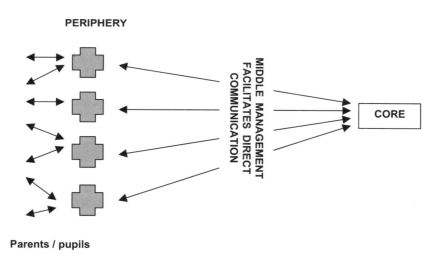

Figure 36. Filter and facilitator styles of middle management

The challenge for all involved is to prepare the school for change: at the core, along the conduits and at the periphery. Experience from schools that have undertaken intellectual capital initiatives suggests that the following steps may offer such a route (see Figure 37):

- The school's mission statement, what it aspires to and believes in, should be formulated with intellectual capital retention and knowledge continuity in mind.
- The school's policy statements and aims should be made explicit and flow as a consequence of the mission statement.

- The strategy (or at least the initial strategy) by which the school hopes to fulfil its mission should be stated as a public commitment.
- Existing structures should be audited, establishing a place for and examining the nature of the school's intelligence and the competencies already extant among staff.
- Shortfalls and surpluses should be identified and hard questions asked about the adequacy of existing processes, and the effectiveness of current staff and the procedures for replacing them.
- Back-end intelligence should be geared for continuity (value retention) and not bundled with front-end intelligence (value creation). The strategy for intellectual capital management should not be compromised by duplication.
- A strategic decision should be made to centralise intelligence that is shared across constituent operations, and decision making should be delegated to the teaching periphery. The extent of stakeholder access to the core should be decided in parallel.
- The school should change from a departmentalised superstructure to a shared modular infrastructure, looking for opportunities to build connectivity and fluidity between existing intelligence modules.
- It is important that every module is, potentially at least, connected to the network. Schools should be aware that isolated parts undermine the whole. In-service training should largely concentrate on avoiding this and on developing a shared protocol for internal communication.

A failing organisation is characterised by an inability to adapt, an unwillingness to learn and inconsistent communications. In schools, this is usually manifested by an increased number of complaints from teachers, parents and students, a decision making process that is perceived as being unresponsive, growing organisational inflexibility, and a failure to meet the reasonable expectations of staff and customers. Whereas networked organisations are structured to encourage effective communications, poor organisations build barriers to it. The cyclical flow of information and feedback suffers thrombosis and boundaries grow between hierarchical levels and between subject departments on the same hierarchical level. However, networked organisations require maintenance too. They may be flatter structures, but flatter structures are not necessary barrier-free. Horizontal (hierarchical) barriers to vertical communication may have been removed, but vertical (specialist-driven) barriers to effective teamworking may remain (see Figure 38). Network managers must remain vigilant and realistic.

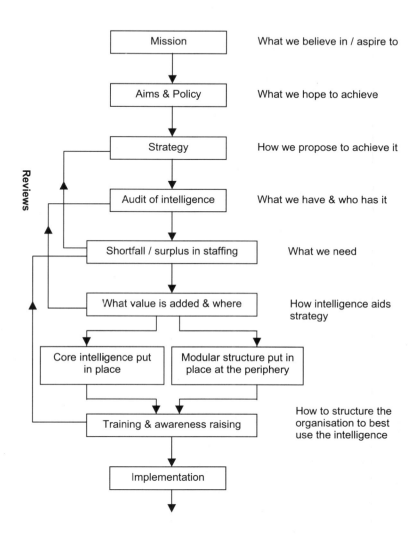

Figure 37. Preparing an organisation for change

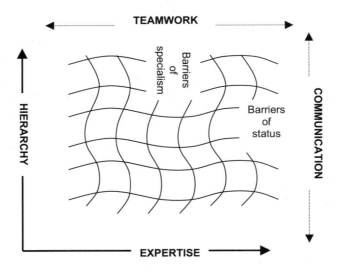

Figure 38. Barriers

To equip schools to survive and thrive in a networked world, internal relationships should make and break around issues and opportunities, rather than around competencies or status. Schools should be characterised by interdependence and reciprocity, with responsibility devolved to autonomous modular groups and individuals who are expected to exercise what could be termed *informed discretion*.

Networked organisations typically adopt a multi-disciplinary approach to problem-solving, achieving outcomes by assembling, disassembling and reassembling coalitions and issue teams. They set unambiguous goals and have a shared sense of ownership. Performance appraisal is done in a transparent manner and teams appraise their own performance relative to other teams in the network. Improvement is achieved through the pursuit of exacting standards, supported by a shared sense of responsibility and mission. Consequently, it is in everyone's interest to eliminate differentials. Communication between individuals and modular groups, typically focused and direct, should take place irrespective of status, function or location.

SUPPORTING NETWORKING WITHIN AND BETWEEN SCHOOLS

An organisation's strategic rationale is influenced by whether it is driven by internal or by external factors. Historically, schools are internally driven and person- focused organisations, concentrating on the human relationships between its elements, albeit with some external influence. As a consequence, schools have tended to develop independently of each other, though this situation is now changing as external factors exert a greater influence on what they do. Networked schools typically allow these internal and external influences to interact relatively freely with many and varied connections being made between the school's constituent parts; they allow social and technological processes to influence each other, while setting a style and culture for improvement.

Supporting school networks with Information Technology

Although investment in it is usually expensive, Information Technology can be hugely supportive of school networks and knowledge continuity management in many different ways:

- Online databases allow stakeholders to identify key people and critical information with a minimum of fuss and run-around.
- E-mail allows contact with a school to be immediate and in real time (assuming other forms of communication are unsuitable).
- Staff communications can be supported by an intranet and stakeholders can be given tiered access if security clearance levels can be arranged.
- Students can use the intranet to track their own progress.
- Administration and financial management can be made more efficient using dedicated software. Quotations, orders, invoices and payments can be made electronically from the core.
- Project teams can work together remotely, especially at planning stages, through electronic conferencing. Since geographical location is no longer problematic, schools can network outside their catchment areas.
- Central data storage can be shared within and across institutions and accessed after office hours, allowing teachers to better accommodate the many different demands made on their time. Information can be made available on demand, subject to appropriate security restrictions, and staff and students can work from home by linking into the system.
- An electronic bulletin board for staff can encourage shared ownership of information and maintain a sense of institutional identity.

Supporting soft networks

Employees also need to make informal connections with each other, especially in person-centred organisations like schools. A networked organisation can support this by providing staff with downtime and a suitable environment for sharing intelligence with colleagues. Such *soft networking* should take place at all levels of a school and cut across both vertical (specialist) and horizontal (hierarchical) barriers. It is not political in the sense of being done for personal advancement, but rather constitutes an alternative informal organisation that allows know-how to be shared. The more know-how is shared, the easier it is to retain.

Informal organisations create alternative power structures. Being 'in the loop' means getting advance warning of important decisions, getting access to expertise and resources denied others, and having a personal facility to pursue opportunity. Soft networking gets things done without having to resort to formal authority. Psychologically, it survives on an expectation of reciprocity; the belief that one will be rewarded for accommodation. It sounds sinister, but is really nothing more than shifting the nature of problem solving from a competitive to a cooperative game.

Continuing professional development

Traditionally, the formal professional development of teachers is aimed primarily at enhancing individual expertise and reinforcing specialism. This emphasis needs to shift if a school aspires to be an organisation aware of its intellectual capital and intent on managing the retention of its know-how through networks. Expertise is developed anyway through participation in issue teams and peer appraisal. In networked schools, it becomes accepted practice for individuals and modular teams to keep abreast of advancements in their own specialism without the need for performance-focused staff development programmes.

Professional development programmes in networks focus on developing leadership, problem solving, communication and participation skills. As Hastings (1993) points out, the nature of an organisation can sometimes run ahead of the ability of individuals to operate within it. People must be given the skills to survive and prosper, and this includes the political skill to acquire critical friends to support individual projects. Individuals and task-centred teams need an understanding of how intellectual capital schools function. This ranges from knowing what resources are available for knowledge development and retention to what steps must be taken to access them. They need to understand how knowledge networks function, what expectation the school has of them and who the key people are in any given situation. They need to be trained in network maintenance; oiling the wheels of information sharing.

Recruiting and retaining (or replacing) teachers who can fit into multi-disciplinary project teams is a process that takes time for any school. It depends on the school having developed mature systems, and individuals having developed (from training programmes) a common language protocol and a shared expectation of excellence.

Ironically, setting up systems for knowledge continuity management aimed at retaining within a school the expertise, know-how and competence developed over the years by staff who for whatever reason are now leaving, has the happy ancillary effect of reducing staff turnover. And even when employees do leave, as inevitably happens, the core retains their know-how.

Individual teachers also benefit from continuity management, despite the extra demands made on them: they work in a more satisfying job, they advance faster personally and professionally, they work flexibly with a wider range of projects and with a greater number of specialisms, they are challenged more, their knowledge and emotional intelligence are treated as organisational assets, and the process of peer appraisal and improvement creates a school culture wherein performance measurement is supportive rather than adversarial. All these things reduce staff turnover.

Schools that are not knowledge-aware, on the other hand, are characterised by the partial vacuums that appear when key personnel leave for pastures new. Departing teachers and managers bring the school's knowledge with them and the organisation has no memory of what they achieved or how they did it.

BARRIERS TO INTELLECTUAL CAPITAL NETWORKING AND KNOWLEDGE CONTINUITY MANAGEMENT

Schools need teachers to create, refine, adapt and implement innovation. Teachers in intellectual capital schools need autonomy more than teachers in traditional schools.

They need (and are typically given) the freedom to take decisions, the will to do what needs to be done and the ability to improve on own performance. Intellectual capital schools also need teachers to share good practice and be able to work constructively together, and this creates a tension that is not always easy to resolve: the confidence necessary for autonomous endeavour to flourish is sometimes undermined by the need to work in teams.

Knowledge workers are driven by the need for recognition. In the past, this has come from the status conferred on incumbents by virtue of their specialism and hierarchical level. So when status barriers are removed, as they must be in a networked intellectual capital school, part of the traditional reward system for teachers disappears with them and a sense of insecurity replaces it. *Network status* becomes the new motivation; a new cross-weave in the fabric of the school as an organisation. It derives from an individual's connections and his or her ability to open doors for others and to collaborate over a wide spectrum of activities. In a networked school, individuals and modular teams are rewarded by being asked to undertake important projects, by being asked for advice and assistance, by having achievements celebrated in public, by having good work publicised, by being asked to represent the organisation abroad, and by gaining access to more resources and greater remuneration (Hastings, 1993).

In traditional organisations, on the other hand, experts only identify with their own areas of expertise, gaining recognition by visibly demonstrating that expertise to others. Typically, they either hide their professional know-how from outsiders to create a *myth of private knowledge*, or they frame the world in terms of what they want to tell rather than what others need to know. Traditional organisations support an ethos of arrogance, removing from experts the obligation to explain to stakeholders what is afoot and why. Such an attitude is a barrier to knowledge continuity and is the antithesis of what intellectual capital networking is all about – sharing intelligence. It provides a cultural veto on change, which many organisations find impossible to overcome and which explains why culture is such an important lever for improvement.

Another barrier to intellectual capital networking and knowledge continuity management lies in the *cult of the maverick outsider*; the teacher as hero achieving the impossible as a lone agent battling impossible odds. Seeking assistance is seen as an admission of failure - of disempowerment even - despite the fact that the myth of the hero innovator is just that … a myth! Most successful innovators in science and industry rely on their ability to mobilise other people in pursuit of their objectives, rather than rely solely on their own efforts (Kanter, 1983); that and not solitude is their defining attribute.

Finally, 'old school tie' type networks are also barriers to effective networking. They occur when informal soft networks degenerate into personal advancement societies. This, rather than organisational advancement, becomes their purpose. They are typically closed and impenetrable to outsiders, and this is what marks them out as barriers. By contrast, effective intellectual capital networks, from necessity and inclination, are open and actively seek out outsiders.

OBSERVATIONS ON TEAM NETWORKING IN INTELLECTUAL CAPITAL SCHOOLS

Intellectual capital networks provide an integrated approach to solving problems and experience suggests that they should build project teams around particular tasks. Teams built around tasks repeatedly evolve and dissolve as old problems are solved and new ones present themselves. Although such a multi-functional and multi-disciplinary approach is the result of a networking culture, a network is in many ways the product of a belief that improvement itself is an infinite series of incremental steps. These steps will sometimes be visible and formally instituted, and at other times they will be invisible and have a very short shelf life. Which it is will depend largely on the nature of the issue around which the team is centred, and the extent of its success will depend on how much its members share an understanding of the fundamental nature of the problem under consideration, assuming it is adequately resourced with a realistic time scale.

A team's mix of expertise and experience, rather than the status of its members, is also critical to success. Individuals should belong to it because they can contribute to its success, not because they enhance its status. Quality moderation within the team is not a hierarchical function, but a peer-imposed one. Members have the privilege of autonomy, but they also carry the burden of accountability and the pressure to perform for the common good. They are driven by the status of success and the need for achievement. Their reward is the status they get out of it, not the status they bring to it.

Of course, not every task in an intellectual capital school needs to be tackled by modular teams. There is still room for traditional hierarchical line management and it would be as silly to complicate matters unnecessarily as it would be to over-simplify them. Teams work better in some areas than others. Obviously, anything that requires cross-functional thinking or is concerned with inter-departmental issues is more suited to teamwork than individual endeavour. Restructuring strategic processes and issues relating to staff development are typical team pursuits. Team endeavours are the ones which shape the future of an organisation and are by their nature complicated. Experience from schools that have introduced knowledge continuity management suggests that modular teams dealing with intellectual capital issues are most successful when they have more than a certain minimum threshold of experience and expertise, and when they are steered by someone with an ability to achieve consensus.

Problems associated with team-working
Some significant problems associated with team working have arisen in intellectual capital-centred schools:

- Teams often fail because management does not support them to the necessary extent. Where this problem has been overcome, it was through canvassing support from critical friends. The most successful projects were the ones that had *sponsorship* from at least one senior manager.
- Some teams find it difficult to agree priorities; failing teams are ones in which individual and collective expectations are mismatched.
- Teams sometimes find it difficult to meet in person, in which case communication can be electronic. This is adequate for basic information transfer, but does not build cohesiveness or encourage a shared sense of purpose. It has been found that in circumstances such as these, participants

forget they are members of a team (Hastings, 1993). Putting a multi-disciplinary group of individuals together and giving them a task does not in itself create a team. Schools embarking on intellectual capital programmes need to be aware that cultural factors may exaggerate the communication problems that inhibit a team's ability to morph into a high performance entity, and that this is often the cause of inertia or resistance to movement in terms of driving forward an intellectual capital agenda.

- Team selection should avoid opinionated individualists whose desire for autonomy outweighs their desire to contribute to the collective. It may appear initially that they can significantly contribute to the successful accomplishment of a task, but the risks far outweigh the potential benefits. Avoid them.
- Badly managed and generally unproductive meetings are a common problem. Teachers need to be trained in management skills and need to be given the opportunity to practise them.
- Sometimes teams can become self-justifying and neglect their duty to relate their work to the rest of the school. Care needs to be taken that the lack of hierarchy in networked schools does not compound the problem.

Managing the network of networks

A school with an ever-changing mix of issue-centred groups, involving different combinations of people at different times, presents senior managers with new challenges in tracking, prioritisation and monitoring. They must, for example, keep track of all projects in progress at any one time; what Hastings (1993) has called a *portfolio of organisational work*. This can best be managed by ensuring that output is linked to strategy and that defunct projects are shut down and staffing reconfigured as soon as possible.

Senior management is also responsible for creating a *learning to learn* ethos within the school, aiming to increase the collective intellectual capital after every project (Argyris, 1999; Hargreaves, 1997). However, putting people together and getting the right mix in a school is something that comes not just from management, but from participating teachers as well. An organisation networked to generate and retain intellectual capital demands that its staff take responsibility, rather than merely accepting instruction.

SUMMARY

Expertise is not solely about knowledge and information; it is about experience and the skill of being able to marry know-how with *know-why*. When individuals or teams of individuals leave an organisation, the organisation must retain a copy of that expertise, though the original leaves with them. That is what knowledge continuity management and intellectual capital retention is all about.

In schools, stored replicated expertise must eventually be moved by teachers from the core to the periphery, where pupils and parents are. Networked schools are best placed to do this effectively and efficiently. Network management is therefore primarily concerned with developing *conscious expertise* among employees; know-how that the holders know they know (or put another way, employees who know what they do *not* know). Conscious expertise is superior to the subconscious sort, because it can be replicated.

The key to the successful transfer of retained intellectual capital for reuse at the periphery of an organisation is that it resides in the network in a format that a common protocol can access. The need for developing such a protocol has been stressed a number of times in this chapter and it cannot be overstated. It is essential to effective communication and allows the efficient diffusion of know-how to take place, although the way in which individual schools and their issue teams access diffusing expertise in practice is limited by the nature of their expertise and the skills of those who have access to it.

The usefulness of expertise should be judged on its value to others, not prejudiced by the value its owner puts on it. Full surrender of expertise to a network allows intellectual capital managers to identify those in the organisation who have the required expertise to work on particular problems. Effective teams can only be put together with this information, tailoring the team to the task at hand and bringing together the right people in the right proportions at the right time. That is the purpose of knowledge continuity network management; to bring surrender of information to storage and back to the periphery again.

CHAPTER 8

Intellectual capital metrics

> These studies fortify one's youth, delight one's old age: amid success they are an ornament, in failure they are a refuge and a comfort.
>
> *Cicero, 106 BC - 43 BC.*

INTRODUCTION

The central concern for those charged with measuring intellectual capital in schools is a threefold one: how to account for collective and individual performance, how to track changes in intellectual capital and how to evaluate how productively it is used. No metric will capture each of these three aspects perfectly of course, since correlations between activity and consequence in education are often hard to find and seldom causal. Nevertheless, a school's ability to measure its productivity and intellectual capital is critical to determining its future, even if there is no single or perfect measure for it.

Productivity - defined simply as the ratio of output to input - is a long-term measure of operational efficiency. In the commercial sector, it is measured as output per unit of labour (including materials and equipment), but that does not have any direct analogy for teachers in schools; too much is unknown. However, if any indicator is to be chosen to measure the importance of knowledge to individual institutions, then the best approaches, which are described below, are undoubtedly those that relate output to strategic priorities.

GAUGING THE ORGANISATIONAL IMPORTANCE OF INTELLECTUAL CAPITAL

Intellectual capital is important to organisations like schools and managers need to understand the role it plays in relation to the performance of teachers. Obviously, the more important intellectual capital is to the success of an organisation, the more investment there should be in it and the more effective its management must be. Its importance to a school can only be measured in terms of proxies like the percentage of employees using (and helping to retain) the school's stock of intellectual capital, the amount of resources given to staff development, the extent to which the intellectual capital well-being of the school is valued and the frequency with which it is reviewed. Such proxy measures can be used to compare departments within a school or to compare schools within a local authority.

The Value Added Intellectual Coefficient and Value Added Measures

The *Value Added Intellectual Coefficient* is a measure of return on investment in thinking capital developed by Ante Pulic at the University of Graz, Austria and the University of Zagreb, Croatia. It is based on the premise that the role of labour is different in post-Fordist companies (Stewart, 2002): whereas in the past a given amount of work consistently produced a given quantity of product, nowadays a given amount of work can achieve various outputs (Pulic, 1999). Labour used to be a commodity whose value depended simply on the number of hours an employee worked, which became a proxy measurement for output and was why workers were paid on the basis of time, but in intellectual capital-intensive organisations like schools, output cannot be properly judged solely from time worked; it must be inferred from things like value added.

The Value Added Intellectual Coefficient is calculated by subtracting non-employee inputs (like expenses) from outputs (like revenue from goods and services). This produces a measure of value-added, which is then divided by total payroll costs[33] to give a coefficient measure of how much value has been added per monetary unit of investment in employees. Although the coefficient is imperfect as a pure measure of investment in thinking capital, it is an acceptable way of gauging the importance of intellectual capital to an organisation like a school: the higher the value added per unit of labour cost, the greater the importance of knowledge to the endeavour.

In the UK, schools now have their own prescribed methods for measuring added value to rival measures like Value Added Intellectual Coefficient. They measure the progress pupils make between Key Stage 2 and Key Stage 3 (i.e. across the first three years of secondary school), and between Key Stage 3 and the GCSE examination (i.e. across the fourth and fifth years of secondary school). The measures are called *Value Added Measures* and are intended to allow comparisons to be made between schools with different pupil intakes. *Value Added Scores* compare Key Stage 3 performance with the median performance for all pupils with similar results at Key Stage 2 (or compares their GCSE examination performance with the median performance for other pupils with similar results at Key Stage 3). Individual Value Added Scores are then averaged to give a Value Added Measure for the whole school.[34] Positive scores

---

[33] Stewart (2002) correctly points out that there is an element of pay that is not an investment in human capital; it is simply a labour expense like electricity or stationery. To get a divisor that more accurately represents investment in human capital, the pay and benefits number should be refined by calculating how much employees' work is devoted to current tasks and how much is seeding for the future.

[34] More detailed information about how value added measures and coverage indicators are calculated can be found in the Value Added Technical Information on http://www.dfes.gov.uk/performancetables/

indicate schools where pupils on average made more progress than similar pupils nationally, while negative scores represent schools where pupils made less progress.[35]

Any calculation of added value involves a subtraction and Value Added Scores are no exception. The inputs and outputs are based on points awarded to pupils on the basis of the following tables (see Figure 39). The input measure (Key Stage 2) for each pupil is calculated as the average point score achieved in the three Key Stage 2 test results,[36] and the output measure (Key Stage 3) is calculated as the average point score achieved in the three Key Stage 3 test results.[37]

Key Stage 2 test outcome (Level)	Points: All 3 subjects (Maths, English & Science)
6	39
5	33
4	27
3	21
Compensatory 2	15
N (not awarded a test level)	15
B (working below level of test)	15
Other (pupil absent, script lost, etc)	*Disregarded*

Key Stage 3 test outcome (Level)	Points: English	Points: Maths & Science
E (exceptional)	57	57
8	51	51
7	45	45
6	39	39
5	33	33
4	27	27
3	21	21
Compensatory 2	-	15
N (not awarded a test level)	21	15
B (working below level of test)	21	15
Other (pupil absent, script lost, etc)	Disregarded	Disregarded

Figure 39. How points are allocated to results at KS2 and KS3

Value Added Scores are calculated by comparing Key Stage 3 scores with the median Key Stage 3 scores for other pupils with similar prior attainment at Key Stage 2. Tables supplied to schools by the relevant government department give the national median Key Stage 3 scores for each Key Stage 2 score. Take the following example (Figure 40):

---

[35] For the KS2 to KS3 Value Added Measures, a result of +1 say, means that on average each pupil at the school made one term's more progress between Key Stage 2 and Key Stage 3 than the median for pupils with similar Key Stage 2 attainment. In the 2002 tables, the top 5% of schools nationally achieved scores of +3.4 or above on the Value Added Measure. The bottom 5% of schools achieved scores of –2.6 and below.

[36] For example, the average point score for a pupil achieving test levels 4, 4 and 5 in English, Mathematics and Science respectively is $[27 + 27 + 33] / 3 = 29$.

[37] For example, the average point score for a pupil achieving levels 5, 6 and 4 in English, Mathematics and Science respectively is $[33 + 39 + 27] / 3 = 33$.

A school has four pupils eligible for inclusion in the calculation, with average Key Stage 2 and Key Stage 3 scores as shown (c.f. second and third columns). The national median average scores for those same Key Stage 2 attainments are known (c.f. fourth column), so the Value Added Scores can be calculated for each pupil (c.f. fifth column).

Pupil	Pupil's KS2 average point score	Pupil's KS3 average point score	Median KS3 average point score for the KS2 average point score in column 2	Pupil's Value Added Score
A	25	36	31	+5
B	25	29	31	- 2
C	27	35	35	0
D	27	37	35	+2

Figure 40. Calculating Value Added Scores for a sample of four pupils

The Value Added Measure for the whole school is the simple average of the Value Added Scores for all the pupils in the school. In the above example, the total of the four individual Value Added Scores is +5, so the school's Value Added Measure is +1.25.[38] (Key Stage 3 to GCSE examination Value Added Measures are calculated in a similar fashion).

There is no need to calculate the final overall Value Added Measure if all that is required is an internal measure of the value added by thinking capital; in other words, the value added per monetary unit of employee cost. It is possible, for example, to base a measure of added value for schools on Value Added Scores, rather than on Value Added Measures, where each individual pupil's Value Added Score is multiplied by the income / funding generated individually by that pupil and the sum divided by the total payroll cost of the school, including pay related social insurance and benefits. It is a complicated measure of return on thinking capital for schools - some would say unnecessarily complicated – but it does have a good provenance and should work as well as the corresponding measure in the commercial sector.

Expenditure on intellectual capital
Expenditure on intellectual capital is a simpler measure of how important knowledge is to a school. Keeping track of spending on knowledge workers, on importing outside expertise, and on know-how enhancement and training can give a fairly accurate indication of the extent to which intellectual capital is core to the mission of an organisation. It is certainly easier than calculating Value Added Coefficients as just described.

In his book *The Wealth of Knowledge* (2002), Thomas Stewart, one of the pioneers of intellectual capital, describes a diagram developed by British Nuclear Fuels Limited for mapping expenditure as part of their quality management procedures. A modified version that takes account of the typology of intellectual capital developed for schools in Chapter 2 is represented on Figure 41.

---

[38] The official score would have 100 added for presentation purposes; in other words, the actual official score would be 101.25.

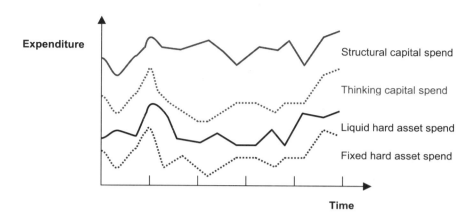

Figure 41. Mapping expenditure on intellectual capital over time

The horizontal axis represents time and a school's major expenditure decision points. As costs are incurred, they are marked on the vertical axis in four parts, which summatively make up the total cost:
- The hard asset elements first, in two parts: fixed hard capital (property, plant, equipment, materials, and so on) and liquid hard capital (cash, manufacturing work, and so on).
- The intellectual capital elements on top of that, in two parts: thinking capital (teaching, research, analysis, planning, marketing, and so on) and structural non-thinking capital (library and ICT spending, staff development and training, infrastructure, and so on).

Admittedly, it is difficult for schools to disentangle and categorise expenditure in this way, but school managers will find it a worthwhile exercise. A diagram like Figure 41 makes it easy for managers to see the relative size of spends - the areas beneath and between the curves - and it can facilitate an effective reduction in expenditure if such is required. It is known from experience in the commercial sector that knowledge-intensive work incurs its highest costs up-front (Drucker, 1999; Stewart, 2002), and diagrams like this can help managers check that costs are dropping off over time, as they should.

IDENTIFYING AND ANALYSING INTANGIBLE ASSETS

One way of identifying and analysing intangible assets, and comparing them with those of other organisations, was developed by Norwegian advertising agency, Bates Gruppen. They developed the notion of *Company IQ*, which Stewart (2002) describes as a numerical non-financial measurement. The first step in calculating Company IQ is to identify what an organisation does that gives it an advantage over competitors; not core skills, but unique aspects to its services or products, like reliability and design. In a management workshop, a list of attributes deemed valuable and unique to the organisation is drawn up, and this then goes to employees and customers as a questionnaire. Each attribute is rated on a Likert scales for *uniqueness* and *value to customers*, and the results are tabulated on a two-by-two matrix (see Figure 42).

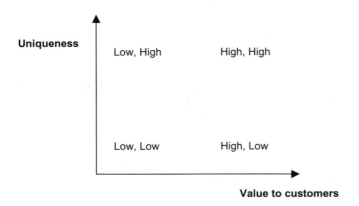

Figure 42. Tabulation of results according to uniqueness and value to customers

The attributes in the High-High quadrant are what everyone perceives to be the most valuable manifestations of the organisation's intellectual capital, and the important thing for management is to discover the knowledge assets that produce them. Another workshop is convened to compile a set of knowledge asset measurements divided equally between the various forms of intellectual capital described in Chapter 2 (see Figure 6). Typically, these will include training costs, the extent of dependence on a small number of employees, customer perceptions, innovativeness and the ability to change, administrative costs, investment in new technology, customer response and turnaround time, measures of loyalty, and so on. The measurements chosen should represent knowledge assets that relate strongly to what gives the company the edge over competitors. They should be measurable on at least a nominal scale and preferably on an interval scale. In this way, comparisons can be made between departments within an organisation or between organisations, with a view to boosting strengths and overcoming weaknesses.

There are other ways to analyse and evaluate knowledge assets. One is *Intellectual Capital Rating*, a concept developed by the Swedish company, Intellectual Capital Sweden. Unlike Company IQ, the results from the IC Rating approach, though quantifiable, are purely subjective and no comparison is possible externally.
How a school differentiates itself from competitors is important to the IC Rating approach too. A questionnaire, adapted for use in schools, is given to managers, teachers, administration staff, parents, students and suppliers. It measures each form of intellectual capital in terms of *efficiency*, *renewal* and *risk* (Stewart, 2002):

- *Efficiency* is scaled from 'extremely good' to 'limited', depending on whether or not the school has efficient processes and high-reputation teachers.
- *Renewal* measures on a Likert scale how strong are the school's efforts to rejuvenate and grow its assets, the number of new services offered, the extent

to which it hires good new teachers, the extent to which it has a rolling staff development programme for existing staff and the number of curriculum initiatives pursued.

- *Risk* is the danger that the school's intellectual assets will lose value as new technologies, societal developments and government regulations threaten its well-being. Risk is graded from 'negligible', through 'moderate', to 'high'.

In the commercial sector, a high correlation has been found between IC Rating and economic growth (Stewart, 2002), but the approach has weaknesses: it does not by itself force an organisation to connect output to specific knowledge; it lacks the facility to make comparisons with other organisations; and it is only as good as the questions asked and the honesty of the answers given. But at least it is easy to apply at the level of the individual school and it can point a clear way forward in terms of remedial action.

EXPLOITING INTANGIBLE ASSETS

Schools must exploit their intellectual capital assets and invest in them to increase their potential for adding value. Rather than look to develop new skills in existing staff or import expertise from outside, schools (which are knowledge-rich organisations) should utilise their own existing skills and experience to link their intangible assets to value-creation (Clare and DeTore, 2000; Stewart, 2002). Knowledge creates value in schools by adding intelligence to the service it provides, by sharing expertise through networks and by improving employees' ways of working (Kelly, 2001). In commercial companies, this can be measured in *options*, which confer the right to do something without imposing an obligation to do it. Options confer a valuable freedom; at the very least, they can buy an organisation more time to make better decisions or lower the cost of learning (Clare and DeTore, 2000; Stewart, 2002).

This concept can be transferred to an education setting without much adjustment. The value of an 'option' to a school, greatest in times of uncertainty, is largely fixed by its time-span; in other words, the time remaining until the option expires in usefulness, like a lease. Certain options, such as the freedom to participate in government education strategies, have specific expiry dates; others, like the fashion for certain curriculum initiatives, have less specific time limits but are limited nevertheless.

The value of alternatives to options has a secondary influence on their value, and options can lose value as time passes. In schools, for example, a curriculum option might seem like an attractive proposition today, but actually exercising it in the future when resources are lower or more urgently needed elsewhere might not be such a good idea. Options can lose prestige due to delays in exercising them and they can impede progress while competitors develop alternatives: there is a price to be paid for the freedom they offer.

Of course, individual knowledge investments in schools can be analysed simply in a ledger-type manner, with the costs on one side and the benefits on the other. For example, an investment in staff training can increase productivity and lower transaction costs, and targeted recruitment and higher entry pay for teachers in key positions can result in immediate improvement and make the learning curve less steep for newcomers. However, it is very difficult to measure on the benefit side how well talent is being exploited at any given time in a school, or how satisfied teachers are in their jobs.[39] One approach in the commercial sector is the *Watson-Wyatt Human Capital Index*, which correlates share value with human relations practices (Stewart, 2002). School improvement research suggests that it could be adapted to an education setting since it is known that improving schools have different human relations practices to failing schools.

The Watson-Wyatt Human Capital Index is based on detailed feedback from over four hundred publicly quoted US companies, who ranked themselves according to some thirty weighted factors: the ability to recruit well, to offer performance related rewards to employees and be transparent with regard to promotions, to sustain integrity in communications, to use resources prudently, to offer job-sharing and flexible working, to encourage a shared sense of ownership among employees, and so on. In commercial companies, these factors have direct correlations with measures of financial well-being like market capitalisation and shareholder return; the higher the Index, the better the company is performing financially.

The results have some important implications for school management. The Index suggests that good recruitment is the most important determinant of success. In fact, every point on the Index's five-point Likert scale equates with a ten percent difference in company value; that is, after controlling for other factors, companies that score 'five' on recruiting have market values ten percent higher than companies who score 'four', and so on down. Anecdotal evidence suggests that recruitment of good teachers to schools is similarly critical.

Other factors have a big influence too: a transparent system of rewards has a nine percent impact on perceived value, a collegial atmosphere and flexible work practices an eight percent impact, and good communications a four percent impact. Somewhat curiously, managing resources prudently does not appear to have any positive impact on the value of an organisation (Stewart, 2002).

Other independent research (Bontis, 1998, 2001 & 2002) has found that nearly seventy percent of the variation in an organisation's ability to recruit and retain good people in key positions is exercised through two factors; leadership and employee commitment. According to Stewart (2002), leadership is the more important of the two because it affects retention both directly and indirectly: people want to work for effective leaders; effective leaders get employees to share and people who share tend to stay together. Bontis also found that the two biggest contributors to thinking capital are employee education and employee satisfaction, but for these to make a difference to value adding, employees have to be engaged directly with customers; in other words, employee satisfaction is an important generator of thinking capital as long as the satisfied employees are engaged directly with customers at the periphery of the organisation. Employee satisfaction and employee commitment are directly related; together they increase the motivation necessary for successful knowledge sharing (Stewart, 2002).

---

[39] Stewart (2002) reports a strong link between employee and customer satisfaction, and the perceived worth of organisations.

MEASURING THE EFFICIENCY OF KNOWLEDGE WORK AND KNOWLEDGE WORKERS

There are two principle ways of measuring the efficiency and productivity of knowledge in an organisation: one is to assess its infrastructure and the other is to assess its vitality.

To have an effective *knowledge infrastructure*, the know-how required for each job must be codified somewhere within the organisation. Stewart points the way forward through work by Speel, Shadbolt and de Vries (1999) and others, by listing some factors critical to the success of knowledge management initiatives. These include having vision, connecting know-how with output, creating a sharing team culture, having adequate resources and appropriate management tools, developing a shared vocabulary, motivating employees with clear objectives, having the support of a critical friend in the upper echelons of the organisation, and having the ability to break through organisational barriers when the need arises. Knowledge management is appraised by asking managers, customers and employees to rate these critical factors on a Likert scale and plot the results on a diagram like the one on Figure 43. The measure is subjective, of course, but it has the benefit of simplicity and it is easy to spot trends (Stewart, 2002).

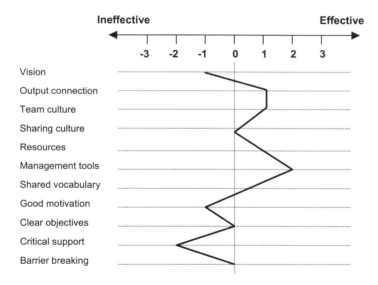

Figure 43. Assessing the infrastructure of knowledge management

Assessing *organisational vitality* as a way of measuring the efficiency and productivity of knowledge is an approach developed by US company, General Electric. Put simply, it measures the talent of individuals in a workforce and differentiates between employees on the basis of performance. Managers rank employees as being in one of three categories, which determine pay, promotion and benefits: a 'top' 20 percent, a 'productive' 70 percent and a 'bottom' 10 percent. The process of ranking the vitality of subordinates forces managers to think about how best to utilise the talent of people working under them (Stewart, 2002). The measurements from many managers in the organisation are then combined and re-ranked to give a measure of the quality of everyone's staff relative to those of other departments. It is a strictly internal measure, of course; the best that managers can hope for is to gauge is how many of their 'top 10 percent' make it into the top 10 percent of the organisation. There can be no comparison with other organisations.

PUTTING A VALUE ON INTELLECTUAL CAPITAL

Stewart's concept of *Calculated Intangible Value* is an attempt to put a monetary value on intellectual capital by means of a *return-on-assets calculation*; that is, calculating the portion of a company's profits it earns over and above its generic activities (Stewart, 1997). Unfortunately, this approach cannot usefully be transferred to not-for-profit organisations like schools because in such organisations, knowledge assets are frequently developed by individuals outside the organisation and no market transaction takes place to analyse. Baruch Lev of New York University has developed an alternative. He infers the value of intangible assets from the returns they produce, dividing profit among various assets until an amount is arrived at that must be attributed to intellectual capital.

The first step in Lev's approach is to estimate the company's *normalised earnings* by taking three years of past earnings and adding three years of forecasted earnings (Lev, 2001).[40] The next step is to see what assets produce these earnings. Hard liquid (financial) capital earns a known rate of interest, as does hard fixed (property) capital, so it is relatively easy to subtract the earnings attributable to financial and physical assets from total earnings: whatever remains must have come from intangibles. And finally, the amount of knowledge capital can be inferred from its earnings by dividing knowledge earnings by the discount rate.[41]

The efficacy of Lev's approach is supported by stock market research; there appears to be a strong correlation between knowledge earnings and performance. Lev's approach can tell managers (and pundits) where to invest and why, but more cautious investors will want to see the approach in operation a bit longer before accepting it completely.

SUMMARY

The importance of intellectual capital to a school can be measured simply in terms of the resources given to staff development, the percentage of employees using the store of know-how, and the degree to which the intellectual capital well-being of the school is valued. A record of expenditure on knowledge workers, on importing outside expertise, and on know-how enhancement and training is the simplest way of gauging the extent to which intellectual capital is core to the mission of the organisation, but

---

[40] Lev gives extra weight to anticipated earnings because the market does.

[41] The discount rate is a proxy derived from the average after-tax profit of the sector in question that depends on knowledge assets to the exclusion of all else. Lev acknowledges that returns on knowledge capital wane over time. After five years, it is assumed that the return declines until after ten years, it reaches the growth rate of the economy as a whole. The discount rate is therefore lower for older knowledge assets.

there are more sophisticated alternatives. The Value Added Intellectual Coefficient is one such. It is a measure of financial return on intellectual capital investment based on the value that has been added to processes by an organisation per monetary unit of investment in staff. In UK schools, the prescribed method for measuring added value based on progress between Key Stages set against a national median of prior attainment allows similar comparisons to be made between schools with different pupil intakes.

The notion of Company IQ is another way of identifying and analysing intangible assets, and comparing them with those of other organisations. The approach identifies what an organisation does that gives it advantage over its competitors. Each attribute is rated by stakeholders for uniqueness and for value, and the knowledge assets that then produce these attributes are sought out by management.

Intellectual Capital Rating is a variation of Company IQ, but unlike it, the results are purely subjective. A high correlation has been found between IC Rating and growth, but the approach by itself does not force an organisation to connect outcomes to knowledge. Both internal and external stakeholders measure each form of the organisation's intellectual capital in terms of its efficiency, renewal and risk, but it is only as good as the questions asked and the honesty of the answers given.

It is very difficult to know how well talent is exploited at any given time in a school and how staff satisfaction relates to organisational attainment. In the commercial sector, the Watson-Wyatt Human Capital Index ranks companies according to various factors that have direct correlations with financial well-being. The results have some implications for school improvement research. They suggest that recruitment is the most important determinant of success. Every point on the Index's five-point Likert scale makes a ten percent difference to company value. Other factors are important too, but to a lesser degree: a good system of rewards has a nine percent impact on value; a collegial atmosphere and flexible work practices an eight percent impact; and good communications a four percent impact.

Research suggests that nearly seventy percent of the variation in an organisation's ability to recruit good staff is exercised through just two factors; leadership and employee commitment. Leadership is the more important of the two, affecting recruitment and retention directly and indirectly: good people come to good leaders and they stay because there are other good people there. In terms of employee commitment, the two biggest contributors are education and satisfaction, but the overall impact is less because for commitment to make a difference to value adding, employees have to be engaged directly with customers. In other words, effective leadership is always good for recruitment and retention, but employee commitment is only good if it acts at the interface with the customer.

The efficiency and productivity of knowledge workers can be measured by assessing the infrastructure and vitality of an organisation. To have an effective knowledge infrastructure, it is a basic requirement that the know-how for each job is codified somehow at the organisation's core, but other factors are important too: having vision, maintaining a connection between know-how and output, encouraging a team / sharing culture, providing knowledge initiatives with adequate resources, having good management tools, developing a shared vocabulary and clear objectives, motivating staff, enlisting the support of a critical friend in the upper echelons of the organisation, having the ability to break through organisational barriers when the need arises, and so on.

Assessing organisational vitality, on the other hand, is an approach that measures the talent of a workforce on a human level. It differentiates between employees on the basis of performance, typically putting them into a category that determines pay and promotion prospects. It is said that at least the process forces managers to think about how best to utilise the talent of people working under them, but it is a rather hard-nosed approach. Results from different departments within an organisation can be combined and ranked to give a measure of everyone's relative worth to the organisation, but it is at best a strictly internal measure.

CONCLUSION

The measurement and management of intellectual capital has become increasingly important to organisations because intellectual capital has become the raw material with which employees generate value in the course of their work. In schools, intellectual capital, rather than physical or financial capital, is the most valuable of all corporate assets. It must be managed and managed well if schools are to realise their full potential.

The nature of value has changed with recent economic developments: management and measurement must change with it. Intellectual capital is now the greatest source of competitive advantage for organisations, and schools are no different in this important respect. Intellectual capital resides in the experience and know-how of teachers, who convert it to value according to their abilities. Effective schooling depends on access to it, so it is only a matter of time before schools, like commercial companies, are rightly expected to report on its development.

APPENDIX

Two-sided mixed-motive games of strategy

Whereas *games of cooperation* are games in which there is no conflict of interest and the pay-offs are identical for both sides, and *constant-sum games* are games in which the sides' interests are totally opposed and what is good for one side is necessarily bad for the other, *mixed-motive games* come somewhere between the two. In a mixed-motive or *variable-sum* game, the sum of the pay-offs differs from strategy to strategy. They rarely produce pure solutions, but they are interesting for the real-life situations they represent and for providing an insight into the nature of conflict and its resolution within organisations.

Four simple mixed-motive games which do not have Nash equilibriums are considered below. A Nash equilibrium is a unique pair of strategies from which neither side has an incentive to deviate since, given what the other side has chosen, that equilibrium is optimal. In many ways, the concept of the Nash equilibrium is a self-fulfilling prophecy. If both players know that both know about the Nash equilibrium, then they will both want to choose their Nash equilibrium strategies. Conversely, any outcome that is not the result of a Nash equilibrium strategy will not be self-promoting and one player will always want to deviate. For example, the game represented on Figure 39 has a Nash equilibrium at (4,4). (In this figure, the first number in any given pair of coordinates represents the pay-off for the row side - Side 1 in this example - and the second number the column side, Side 2). It can be seen that strategy r_1 in always better than r_2 for Side 1 (it is said to dominate it), and strategy c_1 is always better than c_2 for Side 2. So the intersection cell of r_1 and c_1 is a happy equilibrium and neither player has an incentive to deviate from it.

	Side	**2**	
Strategy		c_1	c_2
Side 1	r_1	4,4	2,3
	r_2	3,2	1,1

Figure 44. Pay-off matrix for a two person mixed-motive game with a single Nash equilibrium point

Unfortunately, not every game has a unique Nash equilibrium. The ones that have no Nash equilibrium points at all must be solved using the method of mixed strategies and the ones that have multiple or unstable equilibrium points are categorised according to their similarity to one of the following archetypes.

ARCHETYPE 1 – LEADERSHIP GAMES

Leadership games have pay-off matrices like Figure 40. Since the pay-offs are ordinal rather than interval, the matrix can be made to represent many games, but one example should serve to illustrate its main features.

> **Example 1: A leadership game.** There are two trade unions in a school and each has proposed its own candidate to chair the staff relations committee. Each candidate must decide whether to accept or decline the nomination. If both accept, then the matter will be decided by a potentially divisive vote, which is the worst possible outcome for all concerned. If both decline the nominations, then the divisive vote will be avoided in favour of a third agreed candidate – the second worst pay-off for both, since neither nominee benefits. If one candidate accepts the nomination and the other declines in favour of the other candidate, the accepting candidate benefits most obviously, but the other candidate retains hopes of an unopposed nomination the following year. These pay-offs are represented on Figure 40.

It can be seen from the matrix that there are no dominant strategies. Neither candidate can select a strategy that will yield the best pay-off no matter what the other candidate does. The *minimax principle*, which recommends that a player simply avoid the strategy that leads to the greatest regret, fails too because, according to it, both candidates should choose their first strategy (decline the nomination) so as to avoid the worst eventuality; the pay-off (1,1). Yet, if they do this, both candidates regret it once the other's choice becomes known. So the minimax resolution, (2,2), is not the answer; it is unstable and both players are tempted to deviate from it. (It should be noted that the worst-case scenario, (1,1), arises when *both* players deviate from their minimax strategies).

Despite the failure of both the dominance and the minimax principles, there are two equilibrium points on the Figure 40 matrix. If Nominee 1 chooses to accept the nomination, Nominee 2 can do no better than decline; and if Nominee 1 chooses to decline the nomination, Nominee 2 can do no better than accept. So the strategies with pay-offs (4,3) and (3,4) constitute a pair of equilibrium points.

Unlike zero-sum games, the value of the game is not a constant because the players do not agree about preferability and the two equilibrium points are therefore asymmetrical. There is no formal solution beyond this. Informal factors such as explicit negotiation and cultural prominence must be explored if a more definitive outcome is required. For example, a younger nominee may defer in favour of an older one in schools where seniority is the prominent basis for promotion; or the two candidates may negotiate a political arrangement. Either way, it is in the interests of both players to communicate their intentions to one another and informal considerations are common, which is the opposite paradigm to that which prevails in zero-sum games.

Games with this type of pay-off matrix are called leadership games (Rapoport, 1967) because the player who deviates from the minimax strategy benefits both self and the other player, *but self more* and as such is 'leading' from the front.

| | | Nominee | 2 |
	Strategy	Decline nomination	Accept nomination
Nominee 1	Decline nomination	2,2	**3,4**
	Accept nomination	**4,3**	1,1

Figure 45. Pay-off matrix for leadership games

| | | College | 2 |
	Strategy	Submit preferred calendar	Submit unpreferred calendar
College 1	Submit preferred calendar	2,2	**4,3**
	Submit unpreferred calendar	**3,4**	1,1

Figure 46. Pay-off matrix for heroic games

ARCHETYPE 2 – HERIOC GAMES

Heroic games have pay-off matrices like Figure 41. Again, an example should serve to illustrate the main features.

Example 2: A heroic game. Two colleges in the same conurbation are required, as far as possible, to coordinate their closures so that school buses do not have to run unnecessarily, and they must submit their proposed calendars to the local education authority by a certain date. End of term opening and closing dates are relatively uncontentious, but a major disagreement has arisen over mid-term closures.

The worst-case scenario is that both colleges submit their less preferred options. If both submit their preferred options, then the outcome is not as bad, but far from ideal, since the local authority is bound to arrive at some partially unsatisfactory compromise. Much better if only one college elects to submit its preferred calendar. It maximises its own pay-off of course, but the pay-off for the other college reflects its hope of reversing the arrangement next year. The ordinal pay-offs are displayed on Figure 41.

As was the case with the leadership game described in the previous example, there are no dominant strategies and the minimax principle, in which both colleges choose their first strategy ('submit preferred calendar') so as to avoid the worst pay-off, (1,1), fails. Again, as was the case with leadership games, the minimax strategies are unstable and both players are tempted to deviate from it.

Nevertheless, there are two equilibrium points on the Figure 41 matrix. If College 2 chooses to submit its preferred calendar, College 1 can do no better than submit its less preferred calendar; and vice versa. So there are two equilibrium points with pay-offs (4,3) and (3,4). Again, like leadership games, the value of the game is not a constant because the players do not agree about preferability.

Games with this type of pay-off matrix are called heroic games (Rapoport, 1967) because the player who deviates from the minimax strategy benefits both self and the other player, *but the other player more* and as such is exhibiting heroic unselfish behaviour.

Like leadership games, there is no formal solution beyond this, although it is clearly in the interests of both players to communicate their intentions to one another. Informal considerations suggest that it is a good strategy to convince the other player of one's own determination! For example, if College 2 convinces College 1 that it has a school tour abroad planned which is impossible to cancel, College 1 serves *its own* interest best by acting heroically and choosing its less preferred option (Luce & Raiffa, 1989). It can also be seen from this example that the commonly held notion of 'keeping all options open' is erroneous. Better to adopt a 'no-turning-back policy' or at least convince the other player of one's intention to do so!

ARCHETYPE 3 – EXPLOITATION GAMES

Exploitation games have pay-off matrices like Figure 42.

Example 3: An exploitation game. Nokia and Erickson, two publicly quoted Scandinavian companies in the telecommunications sector, are considering a share issue to raise funds for investment. The financial considerations are complicated by uncertainty over the US Federal Reserve's intention regarding money rates. All other things being equal, it would be better for both companies to wait until the next quarter's inflation figures are known.

The worst-case scenario (financially) occurs when both companies decide to issue shares now, since both will be undersubscribed; the maximum pay-off for a company occurs when it issues shares and the other does not. In such circumstances, market demand would support a high issue price and the issuing company would be perceived among investors as the market leader, though the non-issuing company would also benefit from increased sector confidence. Figure 42 is the ordinal pay-off matrix for the game.

Ericsson

Strategy	Issue shares later	Issue shares now
Nokia Issue shares later	3,3	2,4
Issue shares now	4,2	1,1

Figure 47. Pay-off matrix for exploitation games

Once again, there are no dominant strategies and the minimax principle, in which both companies choose to 'issue later', fails. Although the minimax strategies intersect at (3,3), they are unstable since both players are tempted to deviate from it and both regret their selections once the other's selection becomes known.

The two equilibrium points on Figure 42 are the asymmetric ones with pay-offs (4,2) and (2,4). If Nokia chooses to opt out, Ericsson can do no better than choose the opposite, since to opt out as well would result in the worst possible pay-off (1,1). The converse is true in the case where Ericsson chooses to opt out.

Games with this type of pay-off matrix are called exploitation games (Rapoport, 1967) because the player who deviates unilaterally from the safe minimax strategy benefits only himself and *at the expense of the other player*. In addition, in going after the best possible pay-off, the deviant risks disaster for both.

Even more than heroic games, it is imperative in games of exploitation that the side which intends to deviate from the minimax convinces the other that it is resolute in its intent. Put crudely, the most convincing player always wins exploitation games. In addition, the more games of this sort a player wins, the more likely the player is to continue winning, since the player's seriousness of intent has been amply demonstrated and the player has become more confident. Reputation, the sum of a player's historical behaviour in previous trials of the game, is everything. As Colman (1982) puts it, nothing succeeds like success in the field of brinkmanship! The more reckless, selfish and irrational players are *perceived to be*, the greater is their advantage in games of exploitation, since opposing players know that they risk disaster for everyone if they try to win. This psychological use of craziness can be seen in terrorist organisations (Corsi, 1981), and among politicians and small children, though it should be noted that although the side is *perceived* to be irrational, it is nevertheless acting rationally throughout given its intent to win the game. (Schelling, 1960; Howard, 1966; Brams, 1975).

ARCHETYPE 4 – MARTYRDOM GAMES

Martyrdom games have pay-off matrices like Figure 43. Its most famous prototype is the *Prisoner's Dilemma* game, so-called by A.W. Tucker. It is the most famous and analysed one in game theory, and the example below is a variation on its well-known theme.

Example 4: A martyrdom game. A stockbroker and a company lawyer are suspected of insider trading and are held in separate offices to be questioned by investigators from the Metropolitan Police Fraud Department and the Serious Fraud Office, London. Evidence from colleagues is circumstantial and is not sufficient to convict either party unless one of them incriminates the other. Consequently, investigators offer them immunity and the bonus of being regarded by financial institutions as honest beyond reproach if they give evidence against the other.
If both refuse to cooperate, they will both get off with a reprimand in the absence of any evidence to impose more serious sanctions. If both cooperate, they will both be permanently suspended from trading and excluded from company directorships, but not jailed. If one incriminates the other by cooperating with the investigators, the latter will be jailed and the former will have obtained the best possible pay off – that of having her reputation for honesty enhanced (see Figure 43).

		Stockbroker	
	Strategy	Refuse to cooperate with investigators	Cooperate with investigators
Lawyer	Refuse to cooperate with investigators	3,3	1,4
	Cooperate with investigators	4,1	2,2

Figure 48. Pay-off matrix for martyrdom (or 'prisoner's dilemma') games

This type of game is a genuine paradox. The minimax strategies intersect at (2,2) and suggest that both players should choose to cooperate with the investigators. But unlike the other three prototype games above, this minimax solution does form an equilibrium point, since neither player can do better by choosing another strategy once the other player's strategy becomes known. For example, even if the stockbroker knew that the lawyer was going to cooperate, the stockbroker could not do any better by refusing to cooperate. It can also be seen that the second strategy ('cooperation') for both lawyer and broker dominates. So from every point of view, there is a stable minimax solution at (2,2).

However - and this is the paradox - this dominant solution is worse than the other strategy where both players 'agree' to do the same thing i.e. refuse to cooperate with the investigators (3,3). It appears that there is a conflict between individual self-interest and collective self-interest. Furthermore, the latter strategy where both players optimise their collective pay-offs, (3,3), is itself unstable, since each player is tempted to deviate from it. In other words, in the event of both suspects refusing to cooperate with the investigators, each will regret doing so after it becomes apparent that the other player has also refused to cooperate! It appears that neither the individual self-interest (Nash) equilibrium at (2,2) nor the collective self-interest one at (3,3) offers an acceptable solution.

Games such as this are called martyrdom games (Rapoport, 1967) because if both players deviate from the minimax strategy, they are doing so to benefit *the other as much as self*. And yet, the martyr who defects from this mutuality of martyrdom will always 'win' the game, guaranteeing a better pay-off no matter what the other does!

Martyrdom games have other unique features too. Unlike leadership, heroic and exploitation games, martyrdom games do not have pairs of asymmetric equilibrium points and unlike them too, the worst possible outcome does not occur when both players choose non-minimax solutions. In martyrdom games, both players have dominant strategies and one equilibrium point. If one player deviates from the minimax, he suffers himself (martyr) and benefits the other – the complete opposite of exploitation games. And if both players deviate from the minimax solution, the pay-off is better for both.

Contrary to what is sometimes falsely described as a condition of the game, the players *may* communicate with each other if they so choose (Aumann, 1989). It makes no difference. They might agree to refuse to cooperate with investigators before the game, but they will still choose selfishly to cooperate with investigators when faced with the actual decision, if acting rationally.

It has been suggested that a formal solution to the prisoner's dilemma and other martyrdom games can be found with the help of metagame theory (Howard, 1966). *Metagame theory* is the construction of any number of higher-level games based on the original game. A player is then assumed to choose from a collection of *meta-strategies*, each of which depends on what the other player chooses. What experimental evidence there is supports the theory (Axelrod, 1981). One-off prisoner's dilemma games show a predicted predisposition to selfishness (2, 2); and the results from finitely repeated prisoner's dilemma games, although they reveal a predisposition towards unselfishness (3, 3), can be explained by the somewhat contrived nature of the situation.

BIBLIOGRAPY

Aboud, J.M., 1990. Does performance based managerial compensation affect corporate performance? *Industrial and Labor Relations Review*. Vol. 43 (February). pp.52-73.

Ainscow, M., Hopkins, D., Southworth, G. & West, M., 1994. *Creating the Conditions for School Improvement*. London: David Fulton.

Angelides, P., 2003. *Changing the Structure of Staff Meetings: an efficient approach to staff development*. (Paper presented to the International Congress of School Effectiveness and Improvement, Sydney).

Argyris, C., 1993. *Knowledge for Action: A Guide to Overcoming Barriers to Organizational Change*. San Francisco: Jossey-Bass.

Argyris, C., 1999. *On Organisational Learning*. (2nd edition). Malden, MA: Blackwell.

Arthur, W.B., 1990. Positive Feedbacks in the Economy, *Scientific American*, February. pp.80-5.

Arthur, W.B., 1996. Increasing returns and the new world of business, *Harvard Business Review*. July-August. pp.100-9.

Aumann, R.J., 1989. Game Theory. In: J. Eatwell, M. Milgate & P. Newman (eds) *The New Palgrave: Game Theory*. London: Macmillan. [First published in 1987 as *The New Palgrave: A Dictionary of Economics*].

Axelrod, R., 1981. The Emergence of Cooperation among Egoists, *American Political Science Review*. Vol.75, No.2. pp.306-18.

Barber, M., 2001. High expectations and standards for all, no matter what: creating a world class education service in England. In: M. Fielding (ed) *Taking Education Really Seriously: Four Years' Hard Labour*. London: Routledge.

Beazley, H., Boenisch, J. & Harden, D., 2002. *Continuity Management*. Hoboken, NJ: John Wiley.

Block, F., 1990. *Post-industrial Possibilities: A Critique of Economic Discourse*. Berkeley: California.

Bontis, N., 1998. Intellectual Capital: An exploratory study that develops measures and models. *Management Decision*. Vol.36, No.2. pp.63-76.

Bontis, N., 1999. Managing Organizational Knowledge by Diagnosing Intellectual Capital: Framing and advancing the state of the field. *International Journal of Technology Management*,Vol.18, Nos.5-8. pp.433-62.

Bontis, N., 2001. Assessing Knowledge Assets: A review of the models used to measure intellectual capital. *International Journal of Management Reviews*. Vol.3, No.1. pp.41-60.

Bontis, N., 2002. *Human Capital Study*. Saratoga Institute and Accenture.

Bontis, N., Dragonetti, N., Jacobsen, K. & G. Roos., 1999. The Knowledge Toolbox: A review of the tools available to measure and manage intangible resources, *European Management Journal*, Vol.17, No.4. pp.391-402.

Bontis, N. & Fitz-enz, J., 2002. Intellectual Capital ROI: A causal map of human capital antecedents and consequents. *Journal of Intellectual Capital*. Vol.3, No.3. pp.223-47.

Bontis, N. & Nikitopoulos, D., 2001. Thought Leadership on Intellectual Capital. *Journal of Intellectual Capital*. Vol.2, No.3. pp.183-91

Brams, S.J., 1990. *Negotiation Games: Applying Game Theory to Bargaining and Arbitration*. London: Routledge.

Cheng, Y. C., 1996. *School Effectiveness and School-Based Management: A Mechanism for Development*. London: Falmer Press.

Clare, M. & DeTore, A.W., 2000. *Knowledge Assets Professional's Guide to Valuation and Financial Management*. San Diego, Calif: Harcourt.

Coase, R.H., 1937. The Nature of the Firm, *Economica*. Vol.4. pp.386-405.

Coase, R.H., 1988. *The Firm, the Market and the Law*. Chicago, Ill: Chicago University Press.

Cohen, L., 1995. *Quality Function Deployment: How to Make QFD Work For You*. Reading, Mass: Addison-Wesley.

Cohen, M.D. & March, J.G., 1986. *Leadership and Ambiguity; the American College President*. Boston: Harvard Business School Press.

Cohen, M.D., March, J.G. & Olsen, J.P., 1972. A Garbage Can Model of Organizational Choice. *Administrative Science Quarterly*, 171.

Colman, A.M., 1982. *Game Theory and Experimental Games: The Study of Strategic Interaction*. Oxford: Pergamon Press.

Coleman, P., Collinge, J., & Seifert, T., 1993. Seeking the levers of change. *School Effectiveness and School Improvement*. Vol.4, No.1. pp.59-83.

Corsi, J.R., 1981. Terrorism as a Desperate Game: Fear, bargaining and communication in the terrorist event, *Journal of Conflict Resolution*. Vol.25, No.2. pp.47-85.

Cropanzano, R. & Fulger, R., 1991. Procedural Justice and Worker Motivation. In: R. Steers & L. Porter (eds) *Motivation and Work Behaviour*. (5th edition). New York: McGraw-Hill.

Dalin, P., 1993. *Changing the School Culture*. London: Cassell.

Dalin, P. & Rust, V.D., 1996. *Towards Schooling for the Twenty-First Century*. London: Cassell.

Davenport, T.H. & Prusak, L., 1997. *Working Knowledge: How Organizations Manage What They Know*. Cambridge, Mass: Harvard Business School Press.

DfEE, 1998. *Teachers: Meeting the Challenge of Change, Green Paper Cm 4164*. London: DfEE.

DfEE, 1999. *Performance Management Framework for Teachers*. London: DfEE.

DfES, 2002. *Press release, 23/1/02*. London: DfEE.

Drucker, P., 1982. *The Changing World of the Executive*. Oxford: Butterworth-Heinemann. (1995 printing).

Drucker, P., 1994. *The Effective Executive*. Oxford: Butterworth-Heinemann.

Drucker, P., 1994. *Managing for Results: economic tasks and risk-taking decisions*. Oxford: Butterworth-Heinemann.

Drucker, P., 1999. *Management challenges for the 21st century*. Oxford: Butterworth-Heinemann.

Eccles, R., 1991. The performance measurement manifesto, *Harvard Business Review*. Jan-Feb. pp.131-7.

Fielding, M. (ed) 2001. Student Voice, *Forum (Special Issue)*. Vol.43, No.2.

Fornell, C., 1992. A national customer satisfaction barometer: the Swedish experience, *Journal of Marketing*. pp. 6-21.

Fullan, M., 1991. *The New Meaning of Educational Change*. New York: Teachers' College Press.

Fullan, M., 1993. *Change forces: probing the depths of educational reform*. London: Falmer Press.

Furnham, A., 1993. Wasting Time in the Board Room, *Financial Times*. March 10, 1993.

Garratt, B., 2000. *The Learning Organization: Developing Democracy at Work*. London: Harper Collins Business. [First published in the UK in 1987 by Fontana].

Gurbaxani, V. & Whang, S., 1991. The Impact of Information Systems on Organisations and Markets, *Communication of the ACM*. January 1991. pp.59-73.

Handy, C.B., 1989. *The Age of Unreason*. London: Business Books.

Hargreaves, A., 1992. Contrived Collegiality: the Micropolitics of Teacher Collaboration. In: Bennett, N., Crawford, M. & Riches, C.R. (eds) *Managing Change in Education: individual and organisational perspectives*. London: PCP.

Hargeaves, A., 1994. *Changing teachers, changing times: Teachers' work and culture in the postmodern age*. London: Cassell.

Hargreaves, D.H., 1967. *Social Relations in a Secondary School*. London: Routledge & Kegan Paul.

Hargreaves, D.H., 1990. *Accountability and school improvement in the work of LEA inspectorates: The rhetoric and beyond*. London: ILEA.

Hargreaves, D.H., 1995. School culture, school effectiveness and school improvement, *School Effectiveness and School Improvement*. Vol.5, No.1. pp.115-23.

Hargreaves, D.H., 1997. School culture, school effectiveness and school improvement. In: A.Harris, N.Bennett & M. Preedy (eds) *Organisational Effectiveness and Improvement in Education*. Buckingham: Open University Press.

Hargreaves, D.H., 2001. A Capital Theory of School Effectiveness & Improvement. *British Educational Research Journal*. Vol. 27, No 4. pp.487-503.

Hargreaves, D.H., 2003. *From Improvement to Transformation* (A keynote address to the International Congress of School Effectiveness and Improvement, Sydney).

Hargreaves, D. & Hopkins, D., 1994. *Development planning for school improvement*. London: Cassell.

Heifetz, R., 1994. *Leadership without Easy Answers*. Cambridge, Mass: Harvard University Press.

Hamel, G. & Prahalad, C., 1989. Strategic Intent, *Harvard Business Review*. May-June. pp.63-76.

Hastings, C., 1993. *The New Organisation*. London: McGraw-Hill.

Howard, N., 1966. The Theory of Metagames, *General Systems*. Vol.11, Part V. pp.167-86.

Isaac, R.M. & Walker, J.M., 1988. Group Size Effects in Public Goods Provision: the Voluntary Contributions Mechanism, *Quarterly Journal of Economics*. Febuary,1988. pp.179-99.

Itami, H. & Roehl, T., 1987. *Mobilizing Invisible Assets*. Cambridge, Mass: Harvard University Press.

Jaques, E., 1956. *Measurement of Responsibility: A study of work, payment and individual capacity*. London: Tavistock.

Jirasinghe, D. & Lyons, G., 1996. *The competent Head: A Job Analysis of Heads' Tasks and Personality Factors*. London: Falmer Press.

Kanter, R.M., 1983. *The Change Masters: Innovation for Productivity in the American Corporation*. New York: Simon & Schuster.

Kaplan, R. & Norton, D., 1997. *The Balanced Scorecard*. Boston, Mass: Harvard Business School Press.

Kelly, A., 2001. *Benchmarking for School Improvement*. London: Routledge Falmer.

Kelly, A., 2003. *Decision Making using Game Theory: An introduction for managers*. Cambridge: Cambridge University Press.

Lazear, E., 1998. *Personnel Economics for Managers*. New York: Wiley.

Leuhrman, T., 1997. What's it worth? A general manager's guide to valuation, *Harvard Business Review*. May-June. pp.132-42.

Lev, B., 2001. *Intangibles : Management, measurement and reporting*. Washington, D.C., Brookings Institution Press.

Levine, D.U. & Lezotte, L.W., 1990. *Unusually Effective Schools: A Review and Analysis of Research and Practice*. Madison, WI: National Center for Effective Schools Research & Development.

Luce, R.D. & Raiffa, H., 1989. *Games and Decisions: Introduction and Critical Survey*. New York: Dover. [Originally published, 1957, New York, Wiley].

MacBeath, J., 1999. *Schools Must Speak for Themselves: the case for school self-evaluation*. London: Routledge.

MacBeath, J. & McGlynn, A., 2002. *Self-evaluation: What's in it for schools?* London: Routledge Falmer.

Mant, A.D., 1969. *The Experienced Manager: A Major Resource*. London: British Institute of Management.

Marsden, D., French, S. & Kubo, K., 2000. *Why Does Performance Pay De-Motivate?* London: London School of Economics Discussion Paper.

Megaw Inquiry, 1982. *Inquiry into Civil Service Pay: Command 8590*. London: Stationery Office.

McDill, E.L. & Rigsby, L.C., 1973. *Structures and process in secondary schools: the impact of educational climates*. Baltimore, MD: Johns Hopkins Press.

McGraw, K.L. & Westphal, C.R. (Eds.), 1990. *Readings in Knowledge Acquisition*. New York: Ellis Horwood.

McGregor, D., 1960. *The Human Side of Enterprise*. New York: McGraw-Hill.

McKenzie, R.B. & Lee, D.R., 1998. *Managing Through Incentives: How to Develop a More Collaborative, Productive, and Profitable Organisation*. Oxford: Oxford University Press.

Milkovitch, G.T. & Wigdor, A.K., 1991. *Pay for Performance: Evaluating Performance Appraisal and Merit Pay*. Washington, DC: National Academy Press.

Mintzberg, H., 1994. The Fall and Rise of Strategic Planning, *Harvard Business Review*, May-June.

Mortimore, P., Sammons, P., Stoll, L., Lewis, D. & Ecob, R., 1988. *School Matters: The Junior Years*. London, Paul Chapman. (Reprint).

Noble & Pym, 1989. Collegial authority and the receding locus of power. In: T. Bush (ed) *Managing Education: theory and practice*. Milton Keynes: Open University Press.

Nonaka, I. & Takeuchi, H., 1995. *The Knowledge-Creating Company*. Oxford: Oxford University Press.

Olson, M., 1965. *The Logic of Collective Action: Public Goods and the Theory of Groups*. Cambridge, Mass: Harvard University Press.

Pare, T.P., 1993. A New Tool for Managing Costs, *Fortune*. June 14. p.124.

Piore, M.J. & Sabel, C.F., 1984. *The Second Industrial Divide: Possibilities for Prosperity*. New York: Basic Books.

Polanyi, M., 1956. *Personal Knowledge*. London: Routledge.

Pulic, A., 1998. Measuring the performance of intellectual potential in a knowledge economy. On the web at: http://www.measuring-ip.at/Opapers/Pulic/Vaictext.html

Pulic, A., 1999. *An Accounting Tool for IC Management*. On the web at: http://www.measuring-ip.at/Papers/ham99txt.htm

Rapoport, A., 1967. Exploiter, Leader, Hero and Martyr: the four archetypes of the 2x2 game, *Behavioral Science*. Vol.12. pp.81-4.

Reich, R., 1991. *The Work of Nations*. New York: Vintage.

Roos, J. & Roos, G., 1997. Valuing intellectual capital: the next generation, *Financial Times Mastering Management Journal*. May.

Roos, J., Roos, G., Dragonetti, N. & Edvinsson, L., 1997. *Intellectual Capital: Navigating the New Business Landscape*. Basingstoke: Macmillan Press.

Rowe, K.J., Hill, P.W. & Holmes-Smith, P., 1994. *The Victorian Quality Schools Project: A report on the first stage of a longitudinal study of school and teacher effectiveness*. (Paper presented to the International Congress of School Effectiveness and Improvement, Melbourne).

Sammons, P. Hillman, J. & Mortimore, P., 1995. *Key Characteristics of Effective Schools: A Review of School Effectiveness Research*. London: Ofsted.

Sawhney, M. & Parikh, D., 2001. Where value lives in a networked world, *Harvard Business Review*. Vol.79, No.1. pp.79-86.

Schelling, T.C., 1960. *The Strategy of Conflict*. (1980 edition). Cambridge, Mass: Harvard University Press.

Schön, D.A., 1983. *The Reflective Practitioner: How Professionals Think in Action*. London: Temple Smith.

Scott, C., Stone, B. & Dinham, S., 2000. *International patterns of teacher discontent*. (Paper presented to the American Educational Research Association).

Senge, P., 1990. *The Fifth Discipline: the art and practice of the learning organisation*. New York: Doubleday.

Shadbolt, N., O'Hara, K. & Schreiber, A. (Eds.), 1996. *Advances in Knowledge Acquisition*. Berlin: Springer.

Speel, P.H., Shadbolt, N., de Vries, W., van Dam, P.H. & O'Hara, K., 1999. *Knowledge Mapping for Industrial Purposes.* Available on the web at http://sern.ucalgary.ca / KSI / KAW / KAW99 / papers / Speel1 /

Stacey, R., 1996. *Complexity and Creativity in Organizations.* San Francisco: Berrett-Koehler.

Steiner-Loffel, U., 1996. *Pupils Evaluate School Culture: a photographic approach.* (Paper presented to the European Educational Research Association, Seville).

Stewart, T.A., 1997. *Intellectual Capital: The new wealth of organizations.* London: Nicholas Brealey.

Stewart, T.A., 2002. *The Wealth of Knowledge.* London: Nicholas Brealey.

Stovel, M. & Bontis, N., 2002. Voluntary Turnover: Knowledge management friend or foe? *Journal of Intellectual Capital.* Vol.3, No.3. pp.303-22.

Teddlie, C. & Reynolds, D., 2000. *The International Handbook of School Effectiveness Research.* London: Falmer Press.

Teddlie, C. & Reynolds, D., 2000. *The International Handbook of School Effectiveness Research.* London: Falmer.

Teddlie, C. & Stringfield, S., 1993. *Schools Do Make a Difference: Lessons Learned from a 10-year Study of School Effects.* New York: Teachers College Press.

Tufte, E.R., 1990. *Envisioning Information.* Cheshire, Conn: Graphics Press.

Vail, E.F., 1999. Mapping Organizational Knowledge. *Knowledge Management Review.* Issue 8, May/June. pp.10-15.

Varela, F., Thompson, E. & Rosch, E., 1992. *The Embodied Mind.* Cambridge, Mass: MIT Press.

West, M., 2001. Reforming teachers' pay: crossing the threshold. In: M. Fielding (ed) *Taking Education Really Seriously: Four Years' Hard Labour.* London: Routledge.

White, T.H., 1961. *The Making of the President, 1960.* New York: Atheneum Publishers.

Wray, R., 2003. Telecoms firm returns to roots after Global fiasco, *The Guardian.* Thursday, June 5.

Wysocki, B., 1994. The Wealth of Notions, *Wall Street Journal.* January 22.